The Powder River Expedition Journals of Colonel Richard Irving Dodge

Colonel Richard Irving Dodge, c. 1876

The Powder River Expedition Journals of Colonel Richard Irving Dodge

Edited by Wayne R. Kime

University of Oklahoma Press : Norman

Other Works Written or Edited by Wayne R. Kime

Pierre M. Irving and Washington Irving: A Collaboration in Life and Letters (Waterloo, Canada, 1978)

(ed.) *Raising the Wind: The Legend of Lapland and Finland Wizards in Literature* (Newark, Del., 1981)

(ed.) *Miscellaneous Writings, 1803-1859*, by Washington Irving (Boston, 1981)

(ed. with Andrew B. Myers) *Journals and Notebooks, Volume IV, 1826-1829*, by Washington Irving (Boston, 1984)

Donald G. Mitchell (Boston, 1985)

(ed.) *The Plains of North America and Their Inhabitants: A Critical Edition*, by Richard Irving Dodge (Newark, Del., and London, 1989)

(ed.) *The Black Hills Journals of Colonel Richard Irving Dodge* (Norman, 1996)

This book is published with the generous assistance of The Kerr Foundation, Inc.

Library of Congress Cataloging-in-Publication Data

Dodge, Richard Irving, 1827-1895.
The Power River Expedition journals of Colonel Richard Irving Dodge / edited by Wayne R. Kime.
p. cm.
Includes bibliographical references and index.
ISBN 978-0-8061-5185-4 (paper)
1. Dodge, Richard Irving, 1827-1895—Diaries. 2. Dakota Indians—Wars, 1876—Personal narratives. 3. Cheyenne Indians—Wars. 4. Dull Knife Battle, Wyo., 1876—Personal narratives. 5. Crook, George, 1829-1890. 6. United States. Army. Cavalry, 5th. I. Kime, Wayne R. II. Title.
E83.876.D64A3 1997
973.8'2'092—dc21 97-9315
CIP

The paper in this book meets the guidelines for permanence and durability of the Committee on Production Guidelines for Book Longevity of the Council on Library Resources, Inc. ∞

In memory of my parents,
Raymond Hanna Kime (1911–62)
and
Beatrice Banning Kime (1915–96)

Contents

Illustrations

Preface

THE TWENTY MANUSCRIPT JOURNALS OF RICHARD Irving Dodge form part of the Edward D. Graff Collection of Western Americana at the Newberry Library, Chicago. These journals—the only ones that he is known to have written—range in date from 1875 to 1883 and record his experiences and impressions during four eventful periods in his later years of military service in the plains and mountains of the American West. The six earliest, dated between May 6 and October 19, 1875, are Dodge's private record of his duty as commander of the eight-company army escort to the official Black Hills Exploring Expedition of that year. My edition of the 1875 journals was issued by the University of Oklahoma Press in 1996 as *The Black Hills Journals of Colonel Richard Irving Dodge*. The second group comprises four journals whose entries begin on October 31, 1876, and end on January 8, 1877. These recount Dodge's experiences as commander of the infantry and artillery battalions in the Powder River Expedition under General George Crook. They are published in the present volume, making public for the first time Dodge's account of that military campaign.

The ten later Dodge journals are as yet unpublished. Of these, eight are dated between September 18, 1878, and December 18, 1880, and center upon his activities in establishing and commanding a six-company post in Indian Territory known as Cantonment North Fork Canadian River. The final two, whose entries run from June 23 to September 28, 1883, record his observations as former aide-de-camp to William T. Sherman, general of the army, in the course of that officer's valedictory tour of military installations and major cities of the West prior to his retirement from active service.

Taken as a group, the Dodge journals do not present a continuous chronological record of the years they cover, nor do they focus on a common set of circumstances. Yet they all merit publication, for they deal with matters of permanent historical interest, and they do so lucidly, suggestively, sometimes memorably.

The Powder River Expedition was a decisive campaign that helped end the Great Sioux War, a conflict that has generated a wealth of published commentary. Despite its acknowledged significance, however, the Powder River Expedition has not yet received much attention from historians. The availability of the Dodge journals should help redress that imbalance. These documents contain a rich budget of information about the expedition: its organization, strategies, chief personnel, internal conflicts, and morale. As no other eyewitness has done, Dodge affords insight into the sometimes tense, sometimes uncomprehending, yet often comradely interaction among the diverse social groups that came together under General Crook during these two months on the bleak Wyoming prairie: officers and enlisted men, cavalry and foot soldiers, Indian auxiliaries, and civilian teamsters.

Unfortunately, neither Crook nor Dodge's fellow subcommander, Colonel Ranald S. Mackenzie, Fourth Cavalry, left an account of the expedition other than in official reports. Dodge was the highest ranking officer in the campaign who set down a separate written record of it. What is more, his is easily the fullest, most detailed firsthand account we possess. The published journals of this articulate army officer will surely prove useful to students of the Great Sioux War.

Dodge's journals will also claim the interested attention of nonspecialist readers. They are the products of a vigorous intelligence, a man who enjoyed expressing himself and had a talent for doing so. The journals served Dodge in the field as notebooks for practical data about itineraries, distances, watering places, and the like, but they were also a repository of his private thoughts. They graphically recount key marches, conversations, confrontations, comeuppances; they record the author's observations of the Indians, of the behavior of his colleagues and subordinates, of the bitter weather; they set forth his reflections on the elusiveness of military glory, the qualities of a first-class military leader, the strengths and weaknesses of his own character as he approached fifty. They make lively reading, in part because of the utter candor with which he wrote them. Dodge's personality comes through vividly, and though not without defect it is decidedly engaging and humane. The Powder River Expedition was clearly an exciting professional opportunity and an adventure for Dodge. His day-to-day record of that adventure conveys a full measure of the boredom, confusion, frustration, and exasperation that characterized much of the campaign, but it also communicates the pride with which he pursued his career as a professional soldier, his intense wish to distinguish himself should opportunity present, and his thoughtful interest in events as they occurred.

For courtesies and assistance extended to me as I prepared this book, I am indebted to many persons and organizations, not all of whom are mentioned here. Financial aid came from Fairmont State College, the West Virginia Humanities Council, the National Endowment for the Humanities, and the Newberry Library, to all of which I express grateful thanks. For their support of my applications for research aid, I am pleased to thank Ralph M. Aderman and Richard D. Rust and my good friend Robert G. Masters, library director, Fairmont State College. Eleanore Hofstetter, Wallace and Susannah Jungers, Kathleen Moyne, and Jude Olsen were gracious hosts during my expeditions in search of information. Robert Heffner, Jr., provided expert assistance with the maps, and John Piscitelli with photography. I owe thanks to Sherry L. Smith and Paul L. Hedren for reading the manuscript—especially for pointing out errors and ambiguities in it. Mr. Hedren kindly made available to me, from his own collection, a photograph of George M. Randall, which is printed here for the first time. I am happy to thank him for that gracious gesture as well. I am grateful to Dr. Lys Ann Shore for her valuable assistance as a copyeditor. By their many courtesies and their professional skill in producing this volume, Sarah Iselin and her colleagues at the University of Oklahoma Press have confirmed my respect and regard. Finally, I express a deep sense of appreciation to my accomplished wife, Dr. Alicia M. Kime.

Institutions whose facilities and personnel have assisted me in my research include the Newberry Library, Chicago; the National Archives, Washington, D.C.; U.S. Army Military History Institute, Carlisle Barracks, Pa.; U.S. Military Academy Library, West Point, N.Y.; Beinecke Library, Yale University, New Haven, Conn.; New York Public Library; New-York Historical Society; Columbia University Library, New York City; Rutgers University Library, New Brunswick, N.J.; University of Pennsylvania Library, Philadelphia; University of Delaware Library, Newark; Enoch Pratt Free Library, Baltimore; History Library, Museum of New Mexico, Santa Fe; Northwestern University Library, Evanston, Ill.; West Virginia University Library, Morgantown; Vermont Historical Society, Montpelier; and Fairmont State College Library, Fairmont, W.V. I am especially grateful to Bart Hollingsworth and his assistants at the Fairmont State College Library for their first-class interlibrary loan service, performed always with a smile.

For permission to quote from unpublished or copyrighted material I thank the Newberry Library, Chicago, and the Special Collections Division, U.S. Military Academy Library, West Point, N.Y.

WAYNE R. KIME

Fairmont, West Virginia

Introduction

Introduction

AFTER A RAPID JOURNEY SOUTHWARD THROUGH Deadwood City, in the Black Hills of Dakota Territory, on September 21, 1876, Brigadier General George Crook arrived at Fort Laramie, Wyoming Territory, where he had been summoned for a conference by Lieutenant General Philip Sheridan, his immediate superior.[1] The agenda included review of the just-completed Big Horn and Yellowstone campaign, in which Crook had played a leading role, and planning for a renewed military initiative in the late fall. The farflung operations of the U.S. Army against the Sioux and Cheyenne Indians in this Centennial year had been arduous, costly, and, thus far at least, strategically inconclusive.[2] Yet the two officers agreed that military pressure ought to be kept up against the roving bands. The army might not succeed in crippling the native fighting force through direct

1. An account of the conference between Sheridan and Crook is in Hedren, *Fort Laramie in 1876*, pp. 170–71. See also Hutton, *Phil Sheridan and His Army*, p. 325; and Hutton, "Philip H. Sheridan," in *Soldiers West*, ed. Hutton, pp. 78–99.

2. A recent narrative of the Great Sioux War is Robinson, *A Good Year to Die*; an earlier volume that focuses on military strategy is Gray, *Centennial Campaign*. A valuable contemporary account of the Big Horn and Yellowstone campaign between May and September 1876 is Finerty, *War-Path and Bivouac*. This book, derived from contributions by Finerty as correspondent for the *Chicago Tribune*, first appeared in 1890. Other standard discussions of events during the period include Vaughn, *With Crook at the Rosebud*; Utley, *Frontier Regulars*, pp. 236–79; and Greene, *Slim Buttes, 1876*. For a summary account of U.S. military operations during the war, see Greene, "The Great Sioux War: A Military Perspective," in *Battles and Skirmishes of the Great Sioux War, 1876–1877*, ed. Greene, pp. xv–xxvi.

engagements, but its intrusive presence in the Indians' hunting grounds, with the consequent unsettling sense of vulnerability, ought eventually to convince them that submission to federal authority was their wisest course.[3]

Crazy Horse, one of the two most prominent Sioux antagonists, was expected to pass the winter with his followers along the headwaters of the Little Missouri River.[4] Crook proposed to outfit a fresh command and set out in quest of the chieftain from a base in the Black Hills. Sheridan expressed willingness to accommodate all Crook's wishes in regard to the organization and equipment of the army force, but he overruled the idea of a departure from the Black Hills in favor of a more comprehensive strategy. Two separate columns would attempt to search out the Indians, using as their bases for supply two newly established cantonments. The more northerly of these, on the Yellowstone River near its confluence with the Tongue River, would support a body of troops under the energetic Colonel Nelson A. Miles, Fifth Infantry.[5] The second cantonment would

3. In an interview on September 15, 1876, with Cuthbert Mills, correspondent for the *New York Times*, Crook expressed his hope for an early sequel to the Big Horn and Yellowstone campaign: "Our next objective is Crazy Horse. He should be followed up and struck as soon as possible. There should be no stopping for this or that thing. The Indians cannot stand a continuous campaign. I cannot tell whether we can go on yet. That depends on our getting the things we want. The best time to strike Indians is in the Winter. They cannot remain together in large bodies at that season. The necessities of subsistence compel them to separate, and then is the time to throw a large force on each band and crush them all in detail" ("The Indian Campaign," *New York Times*, October 11, 1876, p. 5). See also "Gen. Crook's Campaign," *New York Tribune*, October 2, 1876, p. 1; Hutton, "Philip H. Sheridan," p. 92.

4. Notable studies of Crazy Horse are Brininstool, *Crazy Horse*; and Sandoz, *Crazy Horse*. For biographies of Sitting Bull, the other most prominent Sioux leader during the war, see Vaughn, *Sitting Bull*; and Utley, *The Lance and the Shield*.

5. Cantonment on the Tongue River was officially established by Colonel Miles on September 11, 1876; for a contemporary photograph, see Hedren, *Traveler's Guide to the Great Sioux War*, p. 76. In 1878 the post was renamed Fort Keogh. The accomplishments of Colonel Miles during this period are recounted in Greene, *Yellowstone Command*. For the officer's own narrative,

be adjacent to the abandoned Fort Reno, along the Montana Trail approximately eighty-five miles north of Fort Fetterman. From that point Crook would lead a search-and-destroy operation of the sort that had won him renown in recent years as one of the army's most successful Indian fighters. The Powder River Expedition, as the latter campaign came to be called, would march from Fort Fetterman as soon as preparations were complete.

Acting under orders from Sheridan, in mid-October Crook traveled the eighty miles northeast from Fort Laramie to Camp Robinson, adjacent to Red Cloud Agency, where Indian unrest threatened to compromise the coming campaign. The influential Oglala chief Red Cloud had recently joined other Sioux leaders in signing an agreement to abandon the claim of his people to the Black Hills region, but he remained recalcitrant and was believed sympathetic to the tribesmen who still resisted the army.[6] He had moved his band to a point beyond military control, twenty-three miles distant from the agency that had been designated to serve him and his people. He had refused orders to return there, and it was assumed that, if opportunity presented, he would assist his Sioux allies in any way possible. Crook directed that Red Cloud and his people should be captured, disarmed, deprived of their horses, and marched back to the agency. He placed the assault force under command of Colonel Ranald S. Mackenzie, Fourth Cavalry, a mettlesome campaigner who had recently been transferred from Texas to Camp Robinson together with six companies of his regiment. At dawn on October 22 an eight-company command under Mackenzie,

---

first issued in 1896, see Miles, *Personal Recollections and Observations*, with an introduction by Robert M. Utley, pp. 216–44.

6. The activities of Red Cloud during the summer and fall of 1876 are detailed in Olson, *Red Cloud and the Sioux Problem*, pp. 224–35. See also Grange, "Fort Robinson," pp. 210–12; Schubert, *Buffalo Soldiers, Braves, and the Brass*, pp. 12–14.

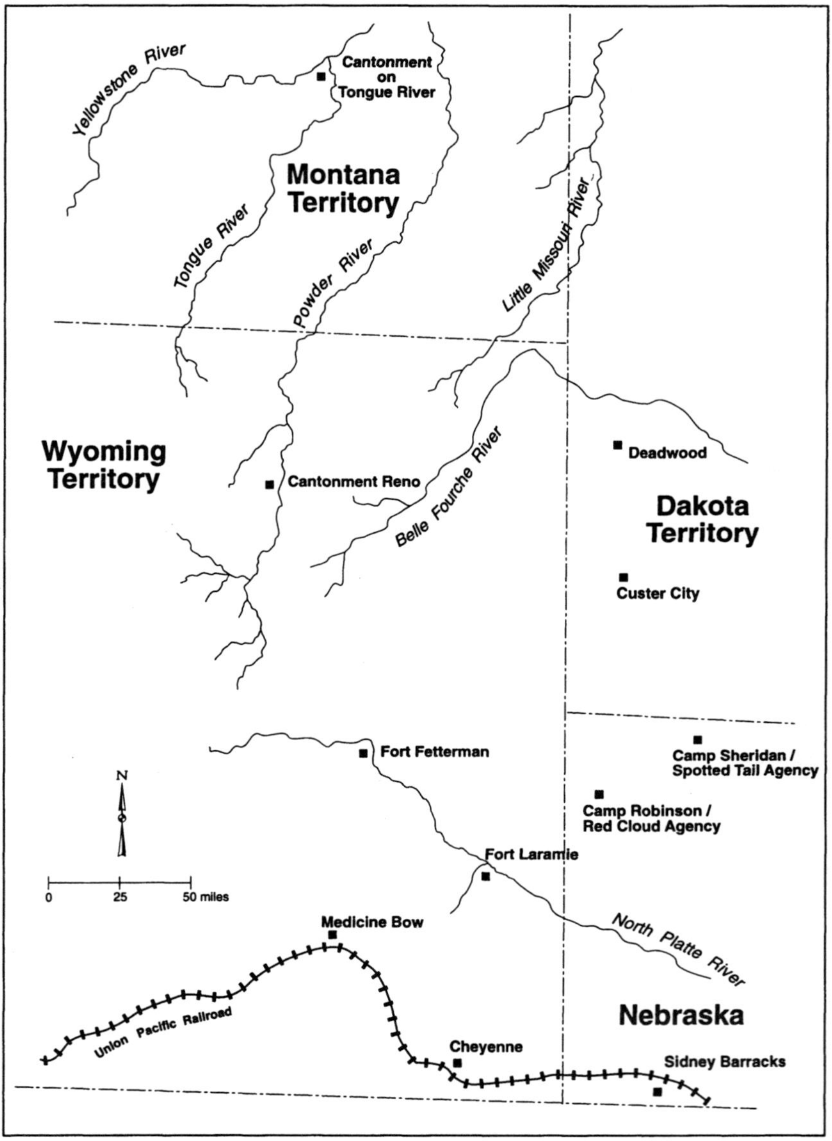

Region of projected military activity, fall 1976

augmented by a contingent of Pawnee Indians who had come north from their reservation in Indian Territory to assist the army, surrounded the camp of Red Cloud and quickly secured a surrender.[7] Crook now took advantage of his position by formally designating a more cooperative Indian leader, Spotted Tail, as henceforward the proper chief of both the Oglala and the Brulé Sioux. In the future, he announced, he would distinguish sharply between his Indian allies and those who flouted federal authority. Indians who submitted to discipline would be permitted to retain their firearms and ponies; some would even be welcome to accompany him on the Powder River Expedition, where they might help capture more of the latter. But those who resisted would lose their weapons and their mounts. By this means Crook secured the services of approximately 150 Sioux, Cheyenne, and Arapaho warriors whose familiarity with the country to be traversed and remarkable powers of observation made them uniquely valuable as scouts. "Some people say it is wrong to use the people of a tribe against itself," he told a newspaper correspondent at about this time, "but pshaw! if I can kill one rattlesnake by making another bite him, I shall do it."[8]

Crook now returned to Fort Laramie, his departmental headquarters in the field, where preparations for the coming campaign were well advanced. By his direction, the Powder River column was to be far better equipped than its predecessor. Sealskin caps, gloves, fur leggings, and felt boots had all arrived for winter use by the soldiers, and thanks to a steady flow of matériel into Cheyenne Depot, Medicine Bow, and other distri-

7. Narratives of Colonel Mackenzie's operation against Red Cloud are given in Nohl, "Bad Hand," pp. 161–68; Pierce, *The Most Promising Young Officer*, pp. 181–84; and Robinson, *Bad Hand*, pp. 202–5. See also Danker, ed., *Man of the Plains*, pp. 194–204.

8. Mills, "The Indian Campaign," p. 4. A useful summary of the motives that led members of various tribes to accompany Crook is in Smith, *Sagebrush Soldier*, pp. 21–23, 34–35, 56.

bution points within reach of Cantonment Reno, the expedition could anticipate a steadier supply of rations, forage, and other necessities than had been available during the summer.[9] Besides regular troops, the force would include 363 native auxiliaries—Pawnees, Sioux, Shoshones, Bannocks, Arapahos, and Cheyennes—organized by tribe into units under the authority chiefly of army officers. Crook was pleased to have recruited scouts from several tribes, believing that their known presence with his command would help demoralize the enemy.[10] The approximately 300 civilian employees who would accompany the expedition consisted primarily of teamsters and drivers under Tom Moore, a seasoned plainsman who had served under Crook for several years as chief packer. The cavalry contingent, which numbered eleven companies totaling 818 men, would be commanded by Colonel Mackenzie, a favorite of General Sheridan. Mackenzie had been present at the Fort Laramie conference in September. The foot soldiers, also a substantial body, comprised fifteen companies, eleven of infantry and four of artillery, 679 men in all. For some reason the officer to command the foot troops remained undesignated until days before the campaign was to begin. The likely nominee had been rumored to be Lieutenant Colonel Richard Irving Dodge, Twenty-third Infantry, who had recently visited Fort Fetterman as president of a general court-martial convened there. On October 31 Crook completed his staffing arrangements by offering the position to Dodge.

9. John Hunton, a rancher in the vicinity of Fort Fetterman who also operated a transportation business employing wagon trains, noted in his diary for September 29, 1876: "Transportation wanted to take 500,000 lbs. supplies to Ft. [i.e., Cantonment] Reno" (*Diary*, 2:147).

10. Telegram, Crook to Sheridan, Camp Robinson via Fort Laramie, January 31, 1877, United States Army, Division of the Missouri, Sioux War Special File, 1876–77, National Archives (hereafter cited as Sioux War Special File). See also Crook's comment to Charles F. Lummis during the Geronimo campaign of 1886, quoted by Utley, "Introduction: The Frontier and Military Tradition," in *Soldiers West*, ed. Hutton, p. 6.

A veteran of almost three decades of army service, the greater part passed in the western plains and mountains, Lieutenant Colonel Dodge was clearly a solid choice.[11] Although he had not yet taken the field in 1876, he knew well the general character of the terrain to be crossed, having earlier been stationed in Wyoming Territory for several years. Dodge's most recent

11. Richard Irving Dodge (1827–95) was admitted as a cadet at the U.S. Military Academy from the state of North Carolina in 1844. Upon graduation from West Point in 1848, ranked nineteenth in a class of thirty-eight, he was awarded a commission as second lieutenant and assigned to the Eighth Regiment of infantry, with which he served on the frontier of Texas through 1856. On March 3, 1855, he was promoted to first lieutenant. From 1856 to 1858 he was on recruiting duty, and for the next two years he served as an instructor of infantry tactics at West Point. Shortly after the outbreak of war he was promoted to captain and began a variety of assignments, chiefly in the recruitment and training of volunteer troops, which won him brevets as lieutenant colonel and colonel. Most of Dodge's service during the Civil War was behind the lines. Not long after commanding his company at First Bull Run, on July 21, 1861, and in the subsequent defense of Washington, D.C., he was assigned to command a camp of instruction at Elmira, New York. He later served as an acting assistant inspector general, as mustering and disbursing agent for the army in the states of Pennsylvania and Maryland, and in other capacities. On June 21, 1864, he was promoted to major, Twelfth Infantry.

Amid the reorganization and reduction in force of the army following the Civil War, Dodge was twice transferred, to the Thirtieth Infantry on September 21, 1866, and to the Third Infantry on March 15, 1869. In February 1867 he was reassigned from Albany, New York, to field operations on the western frontier, where he remained for nearly two decades. Between 1867 and 1869 his duty stations were posts in Colorado, Wyoming Territory, and Nebraska. During that period he established Fort Fred Steele in Wyoming Territory, performed inspection duty, investigated alleged frauds by land claim agents, and participated in operations against Indians. Between October 1869 and July 1871 Dodge was post commander at Fort Lyon, Colorado, and Fort Larned, Kansas. Thereafter, he was a member of a board to revise army regulations, and from June 1872 to November 1873 he commanded at Fort Dodge, Kansas.

On October 23, 1873, Dodge was promoted to lieutenant colonel and transferred to the Twenty-third Infantry. He commanded his regiment and Fort Whipple, Arizona Territory, through July 1874, when the headquarters of the Twenty-third Infantry was relocated to Omaha Barracks, Nebraska. With the exception of his service in the Black Hills in May–October 1875 (see note 12, below), between 1874 and October 1876 Dodge was on duty primarily at Omaha Barracks. Dodge personnel file, United States Army, Adjutant General's Office, National Archives (hereafter cited as AGO); Cullum, *Biographical Register*, 2:217; Cullum, *Supplement*, pp. 193–94; L. R. Hamersley, *Records of Living Officers of the United States Army*, p. 282.

field service was as commander of the eight-company army escort to the official Black Hills Exploring Expedition of 1875.[12] In that operation his skill in conducting troops through difficult country had been conspicuous, as had his executive ability and good judgment. The success of the politically sensitive Black Hills mission was due in large part to the prudent tact he had displayed. Dodge had shown himself a man whom Crook could work with—no small consideration at just this time, when the memory of voiced dissatisfaction and even insubordination among officers and men who had served under the general more recently was still clear.[13]

The opportunity to participate in this perhaps decisive campaign of the Great Sioux War was a stroke of good fortune for Dodge, a gratifying mark of his commander's confidence. Yet it came at a time when he was learning anew that, as he later put it, "domestic felicities and domestic duties are sadly at variance with the active duties of a soldier."[14] His official responsibilities at Omaha Barracks, Nebraska, had been more than mere routine in this eventful year,[15] and the needs of family members had also

12. The fullest firsthand account of this expedition, undertaken between May and October 1875, is Dodge, *Black Hills Journals*; see also Turchen and McLaird, *The Black Hills Expedition of 1875*, which contains Dodge's official report, pp. 30–93. The scientific results of the geological surveying party escorted by Dodge were published in 1880 in Newton and Jenney, *Report on the Geology and Resources of the Black Hills of Dakota*. Works that establish a historical context for the Black Hills expedition are Jackson, *Custer's Gold*; and Parker, *Gold in the Black Hills*.

13. See Vaughn, *The Reynolds Campaign on Powder River*, p. 185; Finerty, *War-Path and Bivouac*, pp. 204–5; Vaughn, *With Crook at the Rosebud*, pp. 165–67; Robinson, *A Good Year to Die*, pp. 253, 262–63; Gray, *Centennial Campaign*, pp. 228, 238–39; Greene, "George Crook," in *Soldiers West*, ed. Hutton, p. 125; Greene, *Slim Buttes, 1876*, pp. 12, 29, 37, 68, 154; Hedren, ed., "Campaigning with the 5th Cavalry," p. 459; King, "Needed: A Re-Evaluation," pp. 229, 232.

14. Dodge, "The Enlisted Soldier," p. 263.

15. In the frequent absence of his regimental commander, Colonel Jefferson C. Davis (1828–79), Dodge was called upon to substitute in that position and also as post commandant. Colonel Davis was on leave from duty December 26, 1875–January 11, 1876; February 28–March 14, 1876; June 26–August 29, 1876; and September 28–October 1, 1876.

repeatedly claimed his attention. His emotionally unstable wife Julia, who resided with him when his postings satisfied her taste for civilized amenities and social contact, was a source of agitation and continuing concern. Additional causes for concern were their seventeen-year-old son Fred and Julia's invalid mother, Maria Paulding. Simply supporting these dependents, while also providing financial assistance to his own parents in North Carolina, a blind sister, and other needy relations, was a challenge, necessitating that Dodge keep a sharp eye out for ways to supplement his $3,000 annual salary.[16] This year, for example, he was engaging in two literary speculations. In April, hoping to take advantage of the public desire for reliable information about the mineral and other resources of the Black Hills region, he had published in New York a slim volume, *The Black Hills*.[17] A more substantial book, *The Plains of North America and Their Inhabitants*, was to be issued in England and the United States in the fall.[18] On August 5 Dodge's domestic obliga-

16. Dodge was the only son of James R. Dodge (1795–1880) and Susan Williams Dodge, who owned a farm on the Yadkin River in rural North Carolina. His sisters were Susan Taylor (b. 1829), Ann Sarah (b. 1831), and Mary Helen or "Sis Molly" (b. 1835); Mary Helen was blind. Aderman, *A Genealogy of the Irvings of New York*, p. 2; Dodge personnel file, AGO; *Official Army Register* (1876), p. 260C; Dodge to William Blackmore, Omaha Barracks, April 16, June 11, and August 2, 1876, Blackmore Papers.

17. Dodge described this work, based largely on his official report, as "given to the public in deference to the general anxiety for a reliable and authentic" account of the region (preface to *The Black Hills*, p. [3]). The text was complemented by eight tinted engravings prepared from photographs taken during the summer of 1875 by A. Guerin, the official photographer of the Black Hills Expedition. A facsimile edition was issued in 1965 (Minneapolis: Ross and Haines).

18. Although this title was Dodge's final choice, it was not used for either the English or the American edition of the book. The English issue was entitled by its editor, William Blackmore, *The Hunting Grounds of the Great West: A Description of the Plains, Game, and Indians of the Great North American Desert* (London: Chatto and Windus). The American text, not issued until January 1877, was entitled *The Plains of the Great West and Their Inhabitants* (New York: G. P. Putnam's Sons). For an account of the discussions followed by lapsed communication that resulted in these two titles being assigned to the same work, see Dodge, *The Plains of North America and Their Inhabitants* (hereafter cited as *PNA*), pp. 21–24.

tions grew yet more demanding when his mother-in-law died and he was named executor of her will, a task that would require his presence in New York for several weeks. He applied for a leave of absence or else some temporary assignment in that city, but the request had not been acted upon by October 31, when the telegram from General Crook's aide-de-camp reached him.

The offer of appointment was thus a mixed blessing to Dodge. He wired his acceptance, and hastily placing some of his personal affairs in the hands of others, with evident excitement he prepared to leave Omaha together with the three companies of his regiment that had been designated for service in the campaign. On the assumption that the weeks ahead would likely be ones worth recording, Dodge began compiling a journal of the same sort he had written during the Black Hills Expedition.[19] Between October 31 and his return to Omaha from the completed tour of duty on January 8, 1877, he faithfully set down, for his own eyes only, his experiences and observations as a participant in the Powder River Expedition. The result, published in this volume, is the fullest firsthand account we possess of this important late campaign in the Great Sioux War.[20]

19. The four manuscript journals describing the Powder River Expedition are among the Dodge Papers in the Everett D. Graff Collection of Western Americana, Newberry Library, Chicago. Dodge wrote his entries in copies of "The Office Scratch Book," produced by H. M. Hinsdill, Wholesale Stationer, Grand Rapids, Michigan. Sturdy and versatile, these inexpensive notebooks were widely used by military officers. They consisted of a stiff cardboard pad at bottom, folded upward and then forward at the top edge and pressed so as to tightly clasp the sheets for writing. The last fold formed a lip that left a maximum writing space of at least 3 3/8 x 4 3/8 inches per page, the pads being manufactured in various sizes. The design of the notebook permitted easy ripping away of individual sheets, which were of cheap, unlined paper.

20. Typed transcriptions of the Dodge journals by a staff member of the Newberry Library have helped two historians to flesh out their accounts of the Powder River Expedition. Smith's *Sagebrush Soldier* centers upon the edited diary of William Earl Smith, her great-grandfather, an enlisted man who served as orderly to Colonel Mackenzie on the expedition. Smith draws upon the Dodge texts as representing the views and experiences of an officer, which were in stark contrast to those of a plain soldier. Robinson makes use of the Dodge journals in *Bad Hand*, his biography of Colonel Mackenzie, for

On November 4 Dodge and the troops with him reached Medicine Bow Station, the stop on the Union Pacific Railroad nearest Fort Fetterman. They then set out on the eighty-four-mile supply trail, encountering along the way several officers and their wives who were passing in the opposite direction en route to new postings. At the fort, where he arrived the morning of November 10, Dodge learned from Crook the details of the expedition's command structure. Unlike Mackenzie, who had been given independent authority over his portion of the wagon train, Dodge would need to rely on the good offices of Crook's quartermaster, Captain John V. Furey, for transportation of the foot soldiers' supplies. The companies placed under his authority would be divided into two brigades, each with its own commander. This arrangement meant the sacrifice of the direct mode of command he was accustomed to, but the idea of functioning in the role of brigadier general under Crook, the field officer—"playing Brig Genl" as he put it—seems to have tickled his professional vanity.[21]

Four days later, on November 14, the column crossed the already frigid North Platte River adjacent to the fort and began the march toward Cantonment Reno. Stretched out for three miles along the valley, on that bright afternoon the troops created a splendid scene. Spirits ran high all along the column as the march proceeded. On November 17, plodding into the wind through a snowstorm, one foot soldier broke into a marching song and was joined by others. Dodge, an infantry officer throughout his career, was proud of his plucky "Doboys." If Crook failed to accomplish something substantial with an outfit like this one, he confided to his journal that night, "he is a very unlucky, or incapable man." First Lieutenant John G. Bourke, Third Cavalry, Crook's aide-de-camp and the

---

their commentary on that officer and on General Crook. For other published accounts of the Powder River Expedition, see note 35 below.

21. Journal One, November 10, 1876.

adjutant of the expedition, was also keeping a diary, compiling his own record of events. Like Dodge, Bourke considered the expeditionary force an admirable one—the best equipped and best officered command he had ever seen.[22]

The presence of native auxiliaries with the expedition was a particular source of satisfaction to Dodge. He shared Crook's somewhat unorthodox confidence in their reliability and strategic value,[23] having confirmed both attributes through personal experience. He was delighted to learn that a leader among the Pawnee scouts was Li-heris-oo-li-shar, or Frank White, with whom he had shared some close scrapes against the Sioux ten years earlier.[24] As an amateur student of Plains Indian culture, he looked forward to these weeks of familiar contact with representatives of various tribes for the further insights they would afford him. Dodge's known interest in Native Americans—approximately half of his forthcoming book on the plains was devoted to commentary on the indigenous peoples of the region—may actually have been a factor in Crook's decision to appoint him. The general liked to surround himself with officers who shared his own respect for the enemy and curiosity about their ways and beliefs. Dodge fit the profile admirably, as did several of his junior colleagues, including Bourke and First Lieutenant William Philo Clark, Second Cavalry. Both these men

22. Bourke diary, November 9, 14, 1876, Bourke Papers. For a biography of this able officer and ethnologist, see Porter, *Paper Medicine Man*; see also Porter, "John G. Bourke," in *Soldiers West*, ed. Hutton, pp. 139–56. Dodge and Bourke were well acquainted, the latter having performed with credit as engineer officer during the early weeks of the Black Hills Expedition. Dodge considered him an "intelligent energetic ambitious officer," and Bourke returned the good opinion (Dodge, *Black Hills Journals*, pp. 18, 97).

23. Crook's regard for Indians as auxiliaries to U.S. military forces was a minority view that he defended energetically. See Crook, *General George Crook: His Autobiography*, pp. 213–14; Utley, *Frontier Regulars*, pp. 53–54, 289–90; Hutton, *Phil Sheridan and His Army*, pp. 325–26; Hedren, *Fort Laramie in 1876*, pp. 91–92, 195–96; Greene, "George Crook," pp. 120–21. For a survey of opinion concerning the safety and utility of employing Indians as military scouts, see Dunlay, *Wolves for the Blue Soldiers*, pp. 59–68.

24. See Dodge, *PNA*, pp. 326–27.

later wrote books on subjects connected with Native American life, drawing upon data gathered in the course of their military service.[25] Dodge himself in 1882 published a wide-ranging account entitled *Our Wild Indians*, which proved extremely popular, selling more than 37,000 copies. In the same year he also published a ringing critique of federal Indian policy, *A Living Issue*.[26]

Colonels Dodge and Mackenzie soon ceased to jockey for the better camping positions at the end of each day's march and, exchanging favors and courtesies, settled into an easy working relationship. From the first, however, Crook was something of an enigma to both his senior subordinates. When in camp the general showed little inclination to fraternize with his fellow officers other than, perhaps, to sit down to a few games of whist. His long daily conversations with the packers, the wagonmasters, and the Indians seemed to indicate a preference

25. Beginning in the early 1880s Bourke (1846–96) won a reputation as an authority on Native American folklore. Among his writings were *The Medicine Men of the Apache* (1882), *The Snake-Dance of the Moquis of Arizona* (1884), and *Scatalogic Rites of All Nations* (1891). Clark (1845?–84) was author of *The Indian Sign Language. With Brief Explanatory Notes of the Gestures Taught Deaf-Mutes in Our Institutions for Their Instruction, and a Description of Some of the Peculiar Laws, Customs, Myths, Superstitions, Ways of Living, Code of Peace and War Signals of Our Aborigines* (1885). Clark traced his interest in sign language to observations he made during the Powder River Expedition.

26. Splendidly bound in red cloth with decorative designs in gold foil, introduced by a letter from General William T. Sherman, and lavishly illustrated, this work was marketed aggressively by its entrepreneurial publisher, A. D. Worthington of Hartford, Connecticut. Its full title was *Our Wild Indians: Thirty-three Years' Personal Experience Among the Red Men of the Great West. A Popular Account of Their Social Life, Religion, Habits, Traits, Customs, Exploits, Etc. With Thrilling Adventures and Experiences on the Great Plains and in the Mountains of Our Wide Frontier.* A facsimile reprint appeared in 1959 (New York: Archer House). For a further description of the original work and its contents, see Kime, "'Not Coarse . . . But Not Delicate'," pp. 79–82.

A Living Issue, published as a pamphlet, consisted almost entirely of text rejected by the publisher of *Our Wild Indians* as too contentious and potentially inflammatory to be included in a volume designed for popular sale.

for their company. Crook kept his own counsel as to his specific plans for the campaign, prompting much uncertainty and speculation. During a day's march he would literally distance himself from the command. Dressed in a canvas hunting costume, he would range two or three miles ahead, sometimes alone, in search of game or else of a glimpse of some new species of bird. His casual exposure of his person to attack by a lurking enemy suggested a disregard of danger that Dodge thought foolhardy and could only compare to the behavior of the late Lieutenant Colonel Custer when in pursuit of glory. In all, Crook's tastes and habits were so far out of the ordinary as at times to mystify his officers. For a short time Dodge was actually tempted to credit the absurd misrepresentation of the general by Reuben Davenport of the *New York Herald*, who claimed that Crook's visible habits of spartan simplicity were all a blind to conceal a private life of sybaritic ease.[27]

Dodge and Mackenzie remained on comradely terms throughout the campaign, neither officer showing an inclination to shine at the other's expense. Still, both men recognized that conspicuous success in the field was a sure path to recognition by their superiors. For his part, Dodge hoped for an opportunity not only to display his own stature as a commander in battle but also to demonstrate what a well-drilled and well-equipped body of foot soldiers could accomplish in a confrontation with Indians. He was sensitive to the slight condescension long exhibited by the cavalry toward unmounted

27. Dodge, Journal One, November 16, 1876. The virulent criticisms of Crook by Davenport during the summer of 1876 are described in Knight, *Following the Indian Wars*; see especially pp. 282–84. That Dodge should credit the allegations of Davenport indicates the degree of his own confusion about Crook at this point. Davenport had accompanied the Black Hills Expedition as correspondent for the *New York Herald*, and at that time Dodge had easily taken his measure. He considered the young reporter "intelligent but ignorant of life, of human nature and a mere child in his contact with the wild Lieutenant [element?] of the plains" (*Black Hills Journals*, p. 58).

soldiers,[28] and from a tactician's point of view he regretted the stepchild role to which the infantry and artillery had often been relegated by the army in recent years.[29] To his satisfaction, within the past few months the strategic importance of infantry had been commented upon publicly as a crucial complement to the speedy cavalry with their short-range carbines. On November 1, for example, an anonymous newspaper correspondent wrote from Fort Fetterman that in a skirmish with Indians "one foot-soldier with his long gun and no horse to bother with, is worth six cavalrymen."[30] It was well known that, amid the privations of Crook's forced march late that summer to Deadwood City, the foot soldiers had easily outdistanced the cavalry with their worn-out mounts.[31] The Walk-a-Heaps, as the Indians called them, were slow but sure.

Dodge had expressed ideas like these to Crook on more than one occasion, and on the day he arrived at Fort Fetterman he did so again. The general, he wrote in his journal, "was very liberal in his allowances" during that conversation, as he had

28. See Knight, *Life and Manners in the Frontier Army*, pp. 96–98. The awkwardness of infantry soldiers detailed as "mounted infantry" to augment a fighting force of cavalry was a comic theme of newspaper accounts. See Vaughn, *With Crook at the Rosebud*, p. 27; and Vaughn, *Indian Fights*, pp. 126–27.

29. See, for example, Finerty, *War-Path and Bivouac*, p. 49; Knight, *Following the Indian Wars*, p. 182; Utley, *Frontier Regulars*, p. 289.

30. Increasing the proportion, this same writer went on to declare that one hundred infantry "will 'stand off' one thousand savages when mounted" ("From the Indian Country," *Philadelphia Press*, November 7, 1876, p. 2, Scrapbook of Mrs. George Crook, Crook Papers). The same article is pasted into Bourke's diary, vol. 16, December 28, 1876–January 3, 1877, Bourke Papers.

31. Cuthbert Mills wrote of the cross-country march toward the Black Hills and of the battle of Slim Buttes on September 9, 1876: "I think there will be no more sneering at infantry in Indian campaigns, at least if they are all like the infantry we have with us. They have won the admiration of every body, both in marching and in fighting. They went into that little skirmish at the village in admirable style, and their long guns soon cleared the Indians from their front. On the march they may be said to have actually walked down the cavalry" ("The Indian Campaign," p. 5). See also Finerty, *War-Path and Bivouac*, p. 49; King, *Campaigning with Crook*, pp. 57, 130; Bourke, *On the Border with Crook*, p. 370; Robinson, *Bad Hand*, p. 102.

been before. Crook could not be entirely indifferent to his subaltern's point of view, for he was himself an infantry officer of long experience. In fact, between 1866 and 1873 he had held the identical position as lieutenant colonel, Twenty-third Infantry, that Dodge now occupied.[32] Even so, as commander of the Powder River Expedition Crook had no plans to deviate materially from a strategy for operations against Indians that he had devised while serving along the Pacific coast in the 1850s and refined in Arizona Territory between 1871 and 1873. Once again he would rely upon a well-conditioned wagon train, supplemented by pack mule transportation, as the guarantor of his force's maneuverability and range. Profiting from some painful lessons learned earlier this same year, he had amassed a much larger complement of Indian scouts than before and had arranged for readier access to ampler supplies. The five infantry companies with which he had set out on the Big Horn and Yellowstone campaign had been increased to the fifteen companies of infantry and artillery now under Dodge. The hardy foot troops would help prolong his presence in the field during winter, and in case of an engagement, they should serve as a steadying influence and constitute a substantial reserve force. What Crook hoped for most was the chance of a surprise raid against the enemy, preferably just at dawn.[33]

32. For the earlier conversations between Dodge and Crook, see Journal Four. These two soldiers became acquainted at least as early as August 1861, when both were captains, Crook having just been promoted to that rank and transferred to the Fourteenth Infantry from his old regiment, the Fourth, which was stationed in California. At that time Crook was in New York City, hoping to obtain a command in the voluntary service. As he later recalled, Dodge was one of those who advised him, if possible, to remain with his old regiment in the regular army, on leave of absence, and thus preserve his lineal rank even as he served with the volunteers—a course he chose to follow (Crook, *General George Crook: His Autobiography*, p. 83).

33. Bourke, *On the Border with Crook*, pp. 130, 158, 284; Greene, "George Crook," pp. 121–22. In an unpublished autobiographical fragment, Crook described his strategy during the Rogue River campaign of 1857, "a system which has been so successful in all my operations against Indians since." The plan included reconnoitering at night while leaving as few signs

In the early days of the expedition Dodge sustained the hope that his men would be called upon to play more than a supporting role. Naturally they would continue performing the varieties of "yeoman service" required of foot soldiers: They would escort pack trains, help transport the sick and wounded, and be assigned routine tasks of various drab descriptions.[34] Still, the latest reports from scouts that the hostiles had retreated into the Big Horn Mountains were auspicious from his point of view, for the presence of the enemy in broken terrain made it more likely that the infantry would have an important part to play.

What proved to be the central incident of the Powder River Expedition began shortly after the force had left Cantonment Reno and was encamped along Crazy Woman Creek, preparing to "cut loose" from the wagon train and move ahead with supplies limited to what could be carried by pack mules. Crook was bound northward in search of Crazy Horse, who at this

---

of his presence as possible, marching against the enemy at night, and attacking by surprise at daylight. "It has been my experience," he wrote, "that nothing demoralizes an Indian so much as surprise and boldness" (Crook Papers). An account by Crook of a reconnoitering action followed by an attack at dawn against the Apaches in 1871 conforms neatly to this pattern; see Crook, *General George Crook: His Autobiography*, pp. 177–78. For a brief discussion of the attack at dawn as "the classic military tactic of the Indian Wars," see Greene, *Slim Buttes, 1876*, pp. 57–58.

34. The phrase is Bourke's in *On the Border with Crook*, p. 285; but see Finerty, *War-Path and Bivouac*, p. 49. Like other correspondents, including those who like himself recognized the strategic importance of infantry, Finerty understood that the cavalry companies were the more likely to see service worthy of his readers' excited attention. In May 1876, when he first reported to Crook at Omaha with a letter of introduction from Sheridan, he was told, "You had better be with the cavalry" (*War-Path and Bivouac*, p. 6).

Rickey, *Forty Miles a Day on Beans and Hay*, provides an excellent summary of the conditions of frontier service for enlisted men but does not address the duties ordinarily performed by soldiers in infantry and artillery units as opposed to cavalrymen. The most suggestive account of characteristic infantry duties on the plains, based on the experiences of Company H of Dodge's regiment, the Twenty-third Infantry, is Paul L. Hedren, "An Infantry Company in the Sioux Campaign, 1876" in *The Great Sioux War*, ed. Hedren, pp. 193–206; see especially pp. 193–94.

time was thought to be hunting buffalo along the headwaters of the Rosebud River. Fortuitously, on November 23 a Sioux Indian, Sitting Bear, brought information that a large village of the Cheyenne tribe lay hidden in the mountains one or two days' journey to the southwest. Sensing his opportunity, Crook at once ordered Mackenzie, with nine companies of cavalry and most of the Indian scouts, to seek out the village and, if possible, destroy it. The result was a raid, shortly after dawn on November 25, upon the encampment of the Cheyenne chief Dull Knife (Morning Star), consisting of 173 lodges situated on either side of the Red Fork of Powder River, which there passed through a rugged canyon.[35] Mackenzie captured more than 700 of the Indians' horses and forced the approximately 250 fighting men of the village to take up defensive positions among stone outcroppings that lined the ravine. The Cheyennes had suffered severe casualties, but they now set up a withering fire from their all but impregnable positions, enforcing a near-stalemate. One U.S. officer and five soldiers had been killed and twenty-

35. The best known account of the Dull Knife battle is Bourke, *Mackenzie's Last Fight with the Cheyennes*. This work was first published in 1890 as an article in *Journal of the Military Service Institution of the United States*. Later in the same year it appeared under the same title as an independent volume (citations in the notes refer to the book, not the article). Other published descriptions of the battle include the newspaper reports of Jerry Roche, cited in note 36, below; De Barthe, *Life and Adventures of Frank Grouard*, pp. 164–71; Danker, ed., *Man of the Plains*, pp. 211–17; Hyde, *The Pawnee Indians*, pp. 336–39; Robinson, *Bad Hand*, pp. 213–23; Smith, *Sagebrush Soldier*, pp. 76–85; Henry H. Bellas, "The Crook-Mackenzie Campaign and the Dull Knife Battle, November 25, 1876," in *Battles and Skirmishes of the Great Sioux War, 1876–1877*, ed. Greene, pp. 167–83. For Indian perspectives on the Dull Knife battle, see Grinnell, *The Fighting Cheyennes*, pp. 359–82; Powell, *Sweet Medicine*, 1:151–69; Powell, *People of the Sacred Mountain*, 2:1009–33, 1052–71; Greene, ed., *Lakota and Cheyenne*, pp. 113–24. Among unpublished firsthand accounts are an address by L. A. La Garde, an army physician who witnessed the battle, given at a dinner of the Order of the Indian Wars, March 6, 1915, Order of the Indian Wars Collection; and a letter, Frank Hopkins to Taylor Hill Hopkins, Fort Duncan, Texas, April 20, 1879, in Indian Wars Miscellaneous Collection. Nohl, "Bad Hand," pp. 174–213, gives a detailed narrative based on several of these sources.

six more men wounded when Mackenzie dispatched runners back to Crook, requesting reinforcement by the infantry. Meanwhile, he burned the tipis in the now abandoned village. These contained almost all their occupants' personal possessions, tons of food, and a large store of military supplies.

The message from Mackenzie reached Crook before dawn on November 26, and by noon that day Dodge and his men, laden with ammunition and two days' cooked rations, had set out across the snow-covered plain. In the eleven hours that followed, the foot soldiers covered twenty-eight miles. For eight of the last ten miles they marched single file through thigh-deep snow along a precipitous mountain trail, their course fitfully illuminated from behind the moving clouds by a ten-day moon. This night march was without precedent in Dodge's career, and not surprisingly his account of it in the journal runs to superlatives. Early the next morning he and his troops hurried toward the scene of action behind Crook and his headquarters guard, but after a short march a messenger appeared bearing an order to countermarch the column. Mackenzie, ascertaining on the morning of November 26 that the Cheyennes had retreated upstream to a point beyond practicable pursuit, had elected to return to Crazy Woman Creek so that his injured men could be properly attended to. All parties thus set course back toward the base camp, Crook reaching it the evening of November 27, Dodge and his men at about noon the next day. That evening, Mackenzie still not having arrived, the two other senior officers met to talk over the affair. Crook's search-and-destroy strategy had succeeded admirably, it was clear. He believed, on the whole correctly, that the blow struck against the Cheyennes was decisive and would shorten the war. He was "well pleased" with the work of the foot soldiers, he told Dodge, even though they had not arrived in time to strike the Cheyennes a yet more crippling blow. But the day belonged to Mackenzie and his cavalry.

Jerry Roche, the able correspondent of the New York *Herald*, had been present at the Dull Knife fight. He wrote enthusiastic accounts of the battle, and newspapers across the nation soon blazoned Mackenzie's success against the Indians as a long-awaited counterstroke after the Custer disaster of June 25.[36] However, for several days after his return to Crazy Woman Creek the protagonist of these narratives was despondent. Betraying signs of the mental illness that was to cut short his career within a few years, Mackenzie bitterly reproached himself for what he considered a clumsy failure, even speaking of suicide. "He talked more like a Crazy man," Dodge wrote after an intense interview, "than the sane Comdr of a splendid body of Cavalry."[37] Gradually the praise of his colleagues, followed by congratulatory telegrams from Generals Sheridan and Sherman, helped lift Mackenzie's depression. Meanwhile, Dodge reconciled himself to the unheralded part he and his men had played. "I only regret that my portion of the Comd had no share or lot in the affair," he wrote upon concluding a narrative of the action as he had pieced it together from participants. "All say that had the Doboys been there not an Indian would have escaped."[38] It was some consolation that fellow officers like Captain James (Teddy) Egan, Second Cavalry, commander of the headquarters guard, were so complimentary. Egan expressed the opinion that the infantry's night march far surpassed anything done during the summer by the much-praised foot soldiers of Crook's column under Major Alexander Chambers, Fourth Infantry.

36. Roche's dispatches include one dated "In the Field, Nov. 25," wherein he reported the rumor "that General Crook, with the infantry, armed with heavy rifles, will be here by to-morrow evening if necessary to resume the contest" ("The Indian War," *New York Herald*, November 29, 1876, p. 7). His subsequent accounts were "M'Kenzie's Victory," *New York Herald*, December 1, 1876, p. 3; and the more detailed "General Mackenzie's Fight," *New York Herald*, December 11, p. 6. As Crook's unofficial press agent, Lieutenant Bourke probably also wrote narratives of the battle for publication in newspapers. However, his articles would have been anonymous or pseudonymous and so, in the absence of corroborative evidence, cannot be attributed to him with certainty. See Porter, *Paper Medicine Man*, pp. 13, 31.

37. Journal One, November 30, 1876.

38. Journal One, November 29, 1876.

Crook now returned his command to Cantonment Reno to re-outfit, presumably for another foray in search of Indians. Dodge heard in a conversation at the sutler's store with Frank Grouard, Crook's recently arrived chief scout,[39] that the expedition would next move eastward to the Belle Fourche River, but the general himself remained silent about his plans. The uncertainty was compounded by a series of orders issued, partially acted upon, and then for no apparent reason countermanded.[40] When the command set out again on December 2, its objective and destination were still matters for conjecture. Dodge had almost made up his mind that Crook had no real plans when, to his surprise, three days later the commander responded freely to an inquiry, spelling out his ideas about the full month ahead. The expedition would first follow the Belle Fourche eastward toward Inyan Kara, a mountain landmark near the northwestern edge of the Black Hills. From that point, depending upon the reports of scouts, it would likely turn north toward the Little Missouri, again in search of Crazy Horse. Emergency rations were to be had at the newly established cantonment on Tongue River, about 150 miles from Inyan Kara. The force would keep the field, awaiting opportunity for a second attack, as long as possible, but Crook expected to return to Fort Fetterman by December 31. Moments after the general had left Dodge's tent, Mackenzie entered it, intent on knowing all that had been said. "I feel a great deal better since Crook unburdened himself," Dodge wrote that night.[41]

39. Owing to illness, Grouard had not accompanied the command when it left Fort Fetterman. He overtook it a few days later and was present at the Dull Knife battle, being one of the men dispatched by Mackenzie to request reinforcements.

40. The secretiveness and seeming irresolution of the commanding officer were noticed by many at this point, and some persons privately recorded their exasperation. See Danker, ed., *Man of the Plains*, p. 220; Thomas R. Buecker, "The Journals of James S. McClellan," p. 30.

41. Journal Two, December 5, 1876. Bourke's diary entry for December 4, the day before the conversation summarized here, indicates that he had learned of Crook's plan (Bourke Papers).

The winter march across country severely tested the skill of the wagonmasters and the strength of the animals. Having ascertained from Dodge that the terrain between the Belle Fourche and Inyan Kara was a desert devoid of drinkable water,[42] on December 5 Crook ordered his commissary of subsistence, First Lieutenant Charles H. Rockwell, Fifth Cavalry, to send for a precautionary three- to five-day supply of rations to be kept at that day's camp. Yet only two days later, the command laid over again to send back for subsistence stores. As in this instance, so in the entire campaign Crook seemed to Dodge unable to coordinate the procedures necessary to accomplish his plan of operations. What was more, even though ensuring the welfare of the pack mules was a key concern in a mission of this sort, the general "might as well be a cavalryman, for his carelessness" about them.[43] On December 8, after an especially demanding day of trailblazing, Dodge remonstrated with him about the civilian packers' casual attentions to the animals. Crook was silent for a moment, then responded only that "he knew the condition of the animals, that he had a certain problem to work out & had to do the best he could with his materials."[44]

42. Dodge had reached this conclusion during his travels through the Black Hills in 1875; Dodge, *Black Hills Journals*, pp. 198, 204, 206, 212.

43. Journal Two, December 7, 1876. Here and elsewhere in his journals, and with a certain relish, Dodge on occasion indulged in disparaging comments about the soldierly capabilities and social habits of cavalry officers. See Dodge, *Black Hills Journals*, pp. 164–65, 166, 168.

44. Journal Two, December 7, 8, 1876. Because the packers operated without the assistance of soldiers, they functioned as a quasi-independent unit (Vaughn, *The Reynolds Campaign on Powder River*, p. 31). Crook's packers were employed by the army quartermaster corps and so were nominally under the authority of its representative, Captain John V. Furey, but they seem to have taken their cues from their own leader, Tom Moore, the general's valued associate. In a testy telegram of November 1879, Crook refused to dispatch Moore and his packtrain for service under Colonel Mackenzie in another military department than his own. "I have been training Moore," he wrote, "for twelve years and I not only need their services but I cannot spare either of them" (Crook to P. H. Sheridan, Fort Omaha, November 20, 1879, United States Army, Division of the Missouri, Ute Campaign Special File, 1879–80, National Archives (hereafter cited as Ute Campaign Special File).

The command reached the Belle Fourche River on December 7, but during the next two weeks it managed to march only thirty-four miles downstream, far less distance than Crook had anticipated covering. Rugged terrain, weakening animals, and worsening weather combined to render the projected move northward all but impossible. Meanwhile, as the commander awaited reports from his scouts and from another group of Indians expected to arrive with intelligence from Red Cloud Agency, the routine business of an army in the field went forward: drills, fatigue details, inspections of equipment, garrison courts-martial. The receipt of mail brought newspapers and—especially welcome in the dreary isolation of the Wyoming winter—messages from relatives and friends. Card playing, hunting, observation of the Indians and their peculiarities, and sociable "gassing" on sundry topics diversified this period of suspended progress across country. Much time was passed writing letters, and on some days Dodge's journal entries alone extended to 1,500 words. A replenished supply of whisky at the sutler's tent threatened disorder in the camp and, in the bitter cold, injury or death by freezing to those who drank too much. A twenty-four-hour guard was placed on the premises, and company commanders were ordered to arrange for distribution of the product to their men by the glass only.[45] One day a Pawnee brought to Dodge as a gift a handkerchief that contained the granulated liver of a just-killed elk, which he indicated would be a tasty treat. Dodge eyed the raw liver, with the contents of the elk's gall bladder sprinkled over it as seasoning, and declined it as graciously as he could. For a moment the Pawnee seemed surprised, but then he proceeded to enjoy the meat himself, consuming the entire contents of the handker-

45. Special Order (hereafter cited as S.O.) 21, December 18, 1876, Order Book, United States Army, Field Records, Powder River Expedition, Headquarters, Infantry and Artillery Battalions, National Archives (hereafter cited as HQIAB).

chief on the spot.[46] On another day Frank White, Dodge's Pawnee friend, appeared at his tent and, after a brief ceremony, presented him one-quarter of a scalp that had been taken from the youngest son of Dull Knife. This observance, Frank White gave him to understand, sealed the two men as something like brothers.[47]

Several of Dodge's journal entries written in camp along the Belle Fourche describe features of the expedition that, as a soldier, he found unsatisfactory and even distressing. Crook's essential weakness, he wrote as early as December 7, was that he possessed "no administrative ability whatever." He effectively cut himself off from the day-to-day business of his command, relying for its performance upon men who, despite his evident confidence in them, were not up to their jobs. Captain Furey, for example, had served as Crook's quartermaster during the summer and apparently had given satisfaction, yet he lacked the snap and personal authority to ensure the smooth operation of a large expeditionary force such as this. He exercised no discipline over the civilian packers, tacitly allowing them to neglect currying their animals at night and even to omit setting them out to graze. On nights when the mules were turned loose to seek forage, they often wandered away, resulting in trouble and delay the next morning for the entire command. Nor, when the army was on the march, did Furey see to it that the wagon train kept pace.

Dodge enjoyed a reputation for easy good fellowship and prided himself on his ability to deal with other men judiciously, but as a commander he expected ready compliance with his

46. Dodge, *Our Wild Indians*, pp. 276–77. Bourke recorded this incident in his diary, dating it December 11 and identifying the Pawnee donor as "Ralph" (Bourke Papers). Possibly he was Ralph Weeks, who had killed and scalped a Cheyenne youth in the Dull Knife fight, thereby earning the Pawnee name Warrior Chief, Lah-we-lah-coo-la-Shar (Danker, ed., *Man of the Plains*, p. 235).

47. Dodge, *Our Wild Indians*, pp. 514–15. See also Journal One, November 30, 1876.

orders, and he had a temper.[48] The maladministration that beset this expedition exasperated him. Once, after a heated exchange with Furey, he counseled himself to say no more, since "there is no sense in making enemies" about matters outside his responsibility.[49] Even so, the foot troops under him all had to bear the consequences of the packers' inefficiency. The situation persisted, and his frustration festered. On December 25, after delays by the teamsters had caused the entire force to wait for hours without food at the end of a march, his aggravation broke out again in an angry scene at headquarters. First he "ventilated" to Crook his views of the packers, "princes in disguise" who apparently valued their own convenience above the needs of the entire command. The general listened for a few moments, then turned away without a word. A member of Furey's staff spoke up to say that nothing could be done; the teamsters were a "ring," and discipline against any one of them would result in resignation by them all. "Let them go at once," Dodge retorted. "I will give you a hundred better teamsters in an hour." This heated riposte, coming as it did from an infantry officer who was sensitive about the subordinate role regularly assigned his men, was not without unintended irony. But it marked Dodge as a professional soldier who respected his troops and subscribed to the view that, as he later expressed it, the "foundation-stone of an army is obedience, its key-stone discipline."[50]

48. In an obituary tribute, Dodge's West Point classmate Colonel John C. Tidball commented on the "many points of good fellowship" that had "made him a marked figure upon the frontier" ("Richard I. Dodge," in *Twenty-Seventh Annual Reunion*, p. 13). Similarly, an earlier obituary notice in the *Army and Navy Journal* began by characterizing Dodge as "a gallant and very popular officer" (June 22, 1895, p. 711). For the displays of temper, see Dodge, *Black Hills Journals*, pp. 17–18, 19, 129n.

49. Journal Two, December 9, 1876.

50. Dodge, "The Enlisted Soldier," p. 261. According to William F. Hooker, who was employed on the packtrains that served Fort Fetterman in this era, little love was lost between civilian employees and army personnel at the post, and the result was "some rather unpleasant experiences for the frontier freighters. . . . The fault probably was on both sides, though I must say in fairness that the army officer who was responsible for discipline had much

In his opinion, the teamsters should never have been permitted to weigh down their wagons with iron stoves, extra blankets, and camp furniture—conveniences all allotted sparingly to army personnel.[51] They should never have been allowed to indulge their own whims and consult their own comfort while the army they had engaged to serve was on the march. Evidently the special perquisites accorded these persons were parts of the "problem" Crook had said he must "work out . . . the best he could."

On December 21, four days before this unpleasant scene, Crook had informed Mackenzie and Dodge of his decision to conclude the expedition. The expected intelligence from Red Cloud Agency had never arrived, the scouts with the command had located no hostiles within striking distance, and with supplies running perilously low, prudence dictated a return to Fort Fetterman. News of the commander's determination was welcomed in camp uproariously. On the return march spirits remained bright even as, on December 23, the weather turned numbingly cold. Assistant Surgeon Curtis E. Price, Dodge's

---

to put up with in dealing with men used to having their own free, wild way" (*The Bullwhacker*, p. 48). A further glimpse of the animosity between soldiers and teamsters in the 1870s is provided in Young, *Hard Knocks*. Harry (Sam) Young tells of a combative quartermaster at Fort Laramie who was thrashed by a sturdy Missourian whom he had been abusing. The quartermaster was cautioned afterward by Captain Andrew S. Burt, Ninth Infantry, to give a wide berth to the teamsters, who were a "hard set" (pp. 159–61). For a discussion of the circumstances that necessitated the army's use of civilian teamsters and the problems of discipline that arose through this arrangement, see Walker, *The Wagonmasters*, pp. 244–49.

51. In General Order (hereafter cited as G.O.) 3, issued at Fort Fetterman on November 11, Dodge had assigned one common tent to every four enlisted men, one Sibley stove to every eight enlisted men, and three blankets to each man (Order Book, HQIAB). See also Bourke's diary entry for November 11, 1876, Bourke Papers. The packers and teamsters were much more fully equipped with supplies and conveniences for their own use. John F. Finerty had noted earlier in 1876 that the packers in Crook's spring campaign "lived far better than the soldiers" (*War-Path and Bivouac*, p. 35). See also King, "Needed: A Re-Evaluation," p. 229.

messmate, recorded temperatures as low as −35 °F, but on more than one occasion the mercury in his thermometer froze, prompting speculation that the temperature had fallen even lower.[52] Encased in layers of padded clothing, Dodge kept up his journalizing habit in his tent at night, recording with interest the discomforts and distresses brought on by these conditions: the impossibility of driving tent stakes, the cases of frostbite, the layers of skin lost when flesh touched metal. "Almost every day a fierce blizzard paid us its respects," Bourke later wrote, "and almost every night saw us bivouac in some spot where water was scarce, alkaline and muddy; fuel scanty and poor; in fact, but grease-wood and sagebrush."[53] At mess one evening, when Mackenzie remarked with satisfaction that the expedition was about to end "without any suffering at all," Dodge took him up at once.[54] There was agreement that the extreme conditions endured by the participants in this campaign would be long remembered.

On December 24 the command welcomed the arrival of Captain George M. (Jake) Randall, Twenty-third Infantry, a respected veteran who was feared to have perished in a mountain snowstorm while escorting seventy-six Crow scouts to Crook's force from their agency in Montana Territory.[55] That

52. First Sergeant James McClellan, Company H, Third Cavalry, recorded in his journal for December 24, 1876, that the "thermometer went to −42 below zero and froze. had to melt snow to make coffee. . . . One man in the Co. had his feet frozen while on guard duty during the night and I can see lots of men riding in the ambulances with froze hands and feet" (Buecker, "The Journals of James S. McClellan," p. 32).

53. Bourke, *Mackenzie's Last Fight with the Cheyennes*, p. 36.

54. Journal Three, December 26, 1876. Apparently without irony, Bourke had expressed a sentiment similar to Mackenzie's in his diary entry for December 20: "We are so very comfortable on this campaign that the whole movement has seemed all a picnic" (Bourke Papers). For Dodge's pleasant variations on the theme of the Powder River Expedition as a picnic, see Journal Three, December 28, 1876. See also Dodge, *Black Hills Journals*, p. 138.

55. The rumor of Randall's death had been widely circulated. See, for example, *New York Herald*, December 22, 1876, p. 5; December 23, 1876, p. 4. Bourke's diary, vol. 17, includes several newspaper clippings that report Randall's death as a probability (Bourke Papers).

evening the general treated Randall and other officers to a social bowl of Christmas punch. Two days later the spirits of all the returning troops were elevated when a large mail packet arrived with a wagon train carrying forage and supplies. Dodge received one letter, from his parents, who were simultaneously anxious about his safety and ambitious for his distinction. Fondly musing on that paradox, he was moved to reflect on the role he and the Doboys had played in the campaign. True, they had not enjoyed Fortune's special favor, but they had done all they could, and "had our luck put us in a fight, we would have made a name for ourselves - or I am mightily mistaken. That's all!" The expedition reached Fort Fetterman under Dodge's command on December 29, Crook having ridden ahead to transact business there before continuing to Cheyenne, where the court-martial of his subordinates in the spring campaign, Colonel Joseph J. Reynolds and Captain Alexander Moore, both of the Third Cavalry, was about to convene.[56]

On December 31 Dodge and his men began the ninety-five-mile march southeast to Fort Laramie, where he had orders to break up the command. After two days on the trail, the now seasoned foot soldiers overtook the cavalry companies, which had left the fort a full day before them. From Fort Laramie he proceeded by ambulance to Cheyenne, where he mixed with the officers assembled there for the court-martial, including its president, Brigadier General John Pope. Two weeks earlier the Twenty-third Infantry had been transferred from the Department of the Platte back to its former station, the Department of the Missouri, which was commanded by Pope.[57] Dodge received

56. On December 26 Crook, Bourke, and others in the command had received subpoenas to appear at the proceedings, which were scheduled to begin on January 5 (Bourke diary, Bourke Papers). A detailed description of the trial is given in Vaughn, *The Reynolds Campaign on Powder River*, pp. 166–90.

57. In 1876 the Department of the Platte included Iowa, Nebraska, Wyoming Territory, Utah, and a portion of present-day southeast Idaho. The Department of the Missouri included Illinois, Missouri, Kansas, Colorado,

from his new department commander the satisfactory news that his next assignment would be as post commandant at Fort Riley, Kansas—a comfortable location likely to please Mrs. Dodge. After an uneventful railroad journey, on the night of January 8 he and his guest Captain Randall arrived at Omaha Barracks. There, after a near-accident as their ambulance approached the garrison, "the greatest danger I encountered on my great winter expedition," they awoke Dodge's domestic servants, had a cot made up for Randall, and went to bed.

The personal concerns that had preoccupied Dodge two months earlier—money troubles, the needs of family members, the executorship—were poised to reassert themselves, now joined by the task of preparing his household for removal to Fort Riley. However, lest his impressions of the winter campaign should grow dim as its events began to run together in memory, he took time to write out a 2,500-word "Resumé" or summary analysis of it.[58] Here he noted that the operation had dealt a significant blow to the hostiles, and acknowledged that General Crook possessed a remarkable power over Indians and was a wily strategist, a tireless campaigner, and a man of courage. Dodge then addressed himself to the single shortcoming that in his view denied Crook stature as "a very great man": a want of administrative ability. Dodge believed that the Dull Knife battle had forever cured Crook of his limited respect for infantry in campaigns against Indians. But he saw no evidence that his former commander would ever be capable of attending with due rigor to all the practical concerns necessary to make good the potential of a military force under his direction. If

New Mexico, and Indian Territory (later Oklahoma). A map of the Military Division of the Missouri, which encompassed both departments and other territory as well, is in Robinson, *A Good Year to Die*, pp. [26–27]. The fullest account of John Pope's later career is a specialized study, Ellis, *General Pope and U.S. Indian Policy*.

58. The undated "Resumé" is Journal Four.

Crook had maintained closer communication with his departmental staff at Omaha, if he had secured the services of a quartermaster who vigorously exercised authority, and if either Crook or Furey had insisted that the teamsters conform to a discipline even roughly approximating what was expected of enlisted men: then the Powder River command would surely have possessed greater range and staying power. For Dodge, the combination of Crook's abstraction from affairs and his quartermaster's lax management had undermined the campaign, which under more effective leadership would "probably [have] struck Crazy Horse."[59]

The ideas expressed in the "Resumé" recognizably grew out of the circumstances Dodge had commented upon during the expedition. More particularly, they recall passages written in the otherwise unproductive days of mid-December when, for amusement and at times to let off steam, he had attempted to set some of his thoughts in order. His beliefs and biases stand out plainly in the "Resumé," and indeed throughout the journals, for inevitably he thought and wrote from a distinct point of view—one that he was at no pains to conceal.

Dodge's opinions about the expedition and its commander were strong and vigorously expressed, but they were far from eccentric. For example, almost all his main points for discussion about General Crook, including both praise and criticism, had previously been voiced by other persons, sometimes in public. Crook was generally regarded as taciturn and awkward in his social manner. His habit of fraternizing with packers and Indians had earlier raised eyebrows, as had his uncommunicativeness about his plans.[60] His efficiency as a coordinator of

59. Journal Four.

60. See, for example, *Army and Navy Journal*, May 8, 1875, p. 613 (hereafter cited as *ANJ*); Finerty, *War-Path and Bivouac*, pp. 55–56; Bourke, *On the Border with Crook*, p. 109; Gray, *Centennial Campaign*, pp. 111, 228. An exception to this standard profile of Crook is found in a memoir of him by Captain Azor Nickerson, who served for thirteen years as his senior aide-de-camp: "To most persons, he appeared to be stern, stoical and sometimes

military campaigns had also been called into question, notably in the summer just past when, in the opinion of some, his poor planning had resulted in needless suffering by his men.[61] His executive skill was soon to be faulted again, and this time by no lesser authorities than Generals Sheridan and Sherman.[62]

The one feature in Dodge's analysis of Crook that stands out sharply from the views of others is his assertion that, especially in the later parts of the campaign, the general paid no close attention to the condition of his pack team or to the work of the men who tended it. Dodge considered the packers' lax performance "a most infernal outrage" which "would not have been tolerated an instant, by any Comdg officer that I know of except Genl Crook."[63] Lieutenant Bourke, from whose writings our ideas of the Powder River Expedition have chiefly been derived, viewed the relationship between Crook and the transportation corps quite differently. In his own diary entry for December 22, only three days before the heated discussion between Dodge and the quartermaster's staff, Bourke wrote that "in winter as in summer and spring, our packers under the able supervision of Tom Moore, have attended with an assiduity almost devotion to the wants of the animals under their care."[64]

---

even stubborn. In reality, he was gentle, genial, yielding and sympathetic. If his surroundings were uncongenial, he was silent, sombre and taciturn. Take away the depressing or irritating element, and he immediately became cheerful and playfully talkative" ("Major General George Crook and the Indians," typescript, Crook-Kennan Papers).

61. See especially *New York Herald*, July 16, 1876, and October 2, 1876, cited in Knight, *Following the Indian Wars*, pp. 241, 260; Finerty, *War-Path and Bivouac*, pp. 179–80, 204–5; Vaughn, *With Crook at the Rosebud*, pp. 160, 228–29; Vaughn, *The Reynolds Campaign on Powder River*, pp. 173, 176; Gray, *Centennial Campaign*, p. 228; Greene, *Slim Buttes, 1876*, pp. 12, 37, 112–13; Greene, "George Crook," p. 125.

62. See William T. Sherman to P. H. Sheridan, Washington, D.C., February 2, 1877, Sioux War Special File; Hutton, *Phil Sheridan and His Army*, p. 327.

63. Journal Four.

64. Bourke prefaced this statement by observing, accurately, that "our pack-train has frequently received my favorable notice in these pages" (diary, December 22, 1876, Bourke Papers).

Later, in *Mackenzie's Last Fight with the Cheyennes* (1890), a narrative chiefly of the Dull Knife battle based upon his diary, Bourke characterized Crook as "the apostle of the military pack-train," praising him for introducing "promptness and discipline" to pack mule transportation.[65] Comparable statements appeared in Bourke's *On the Border with Crook* (1891), a wide-ranging account of events between 1870 and the death of the general in 1890.[66] Dodge's consternation at the behavior of the civilian packers, expressed repeatedly in his journals and also registered to Crook and others, must call into question the accuracy of Bourke's representations on these points.

Bourke surely had no intention to mislead, yet as Crook's trusted aide-de-camp he naturally viewed events and issues from a point of view sympathetic to his commander, whom he was proud to serve as confidant, amanuensis, and informal press agent. His diary, his anonymous newspaper articles, and his later published writings all manifest the desire of an admiring subordinate to support Crook, placing in a positive light what others might regard as eccentricities or faults.[67] Dodge, on the

65. *Mackenzie's Last Fight with the Cheyennes*, p. 14. On pp. 40–41 of this work Bourke repeats almost verbatim the two statements from his diary entry for December 22, 1876. Similar correspondences occur between the carefully phrased texts of Bourke's diaries and passages in his *On the Border with Crook*. Evidently he kept his diary with an eye toward future use of at least some of its entries in published writings.

66. See *On the Border with Crook*, pp. 138, 150, 154, 166, 244.

67. Likening Bourke to James Boswell, the admiring younger companion of Dr. Samuel Johnson who assiduously collected information about the great man for future use in his *Life* (1791), Oliver Knight refers to the young aide-decamp as "Crook's Boswell" (*Life and Manners in the Frontier Army*, p. 27). See also Porter, *Paper Medicine Man*, pp. 12–13; Porter, "John G. Bourke," p. 140; King, "Needed: A Re-Evaluation," pp. 223, 235. A representative instance of Bourke's instinct to support Crook occurs in his diary entry for December 20, 1876, the day before the general revealed to Dodge and Mackenzie his decision to end the expedition: "Had we only enough forage for our animals, we might strike across country and hit those fellows another blow, on the Rosebud; but what can we do, without either rations for men or forage for animals? General Crook has vainly essayed all that ingenuity could suggest to overcome this obstacle, but with utter failure as the only recompense for his exertions" (Bourke Papers).

other hand, had no such motivation. Early in the expedition he was asked by Major Thaddeus H. Stanton, Crook's faithful troubleshooter and journalistic advocate, to serve as a newspaper correspondent and thereby, it was surely understood, portray the expedition in a generally supportive manner, but he declined.[68] Dodge's journals demonstrate at many points his willingness to grant credit wherever he thought it due, but he felt no obligation to praise Crook's policies, extol his character, or gloss over his faults. His aims as a journal writer were private and personal: to record what he saw and experienced during the campaign and, in the undated "Resumé," to arrive at a summary view. Later, at a few points in *Our Wild Indians*, he did portray Crook favorably, but in those passages he made minimal use of the Powder River journals.[69]

During the early months of 1877 General Crook and Lieutenant Colonel Dodge both received popular applause for their quite different recent accomplishments in connection with plains Indians. In the late winter and spring the Cheyennes, and at last Crazy Horse and his people, turned themselves in at the agencies, bringing to an end the Great Sioux War that had tasked the U.S. Army for more than a year. Crook, having proven himself among the most effective of the Indians' adversaries, was fittingly present at Red Cloud Agency to receive some of the incoming bands. For his part, Dodge enjoyed a period of celebrity as author of the newly released

68. Journal One, November 18, 1876. During the spring campaign Stanton had accompanied Crook's command, serving as a newspaper correspondent. During the summer months he was also active in enlisting newspaper reporters who he thought would be sympathetic to Crook. Charles King referred to him as "our polemical paymaster" (*Campaigning with Crook*, p. 26). Stanton's request to Dodge was apparently a continuation of his public relations effort. At the Reynolds-Moore trial, Major Stanton received an official rebuke for his newspaper advocacy of Crook, as did Crook for permitting him to engage in it (Vaughn, *The Reynolds Campaign on Powder River*, p. 178). Yet the general was by no means the only military leader of the era to provide himself with newspaper partisans; the practice was widespread.

69. See Dodge, *Our Wild Indians*, pp. 85, 492, 493–97.

Plains of North America and Their Inhabitants, a volume warmly greeted as the best written and most authoritative popular account yet available concerning the environment, animals, and indigenous peoples of the American plains.[70]

Dodge's career prospered under General Pope, whose orderly habits of mind and pragmatic style as a commander suited him well. In December 1878 Pope entrusted to him a position then of considerable importance, as founder and commander of a six-company post, Cantonment North Fork Canadian River, midway between Forts Reno and Supply, in Indian Territory. In that assignment Dodge's administrative capacity, skill as a plainsman, instinct for diplomacy, and knowledge of the native peoples all came into play. With characteristic lack of fanfare, at the cantonment he resisted the efforts of U.S. citizens to lay claim to Indian lands south of the Kansas state line, worked on behalf of the tribes living in proximity to his post, stood guard against agitation or escape by disaffected Indians in the region, and meanwhile regulated the passage northward through Indian Territory of great cattle herds bound toward Dodge City and Wichita, Kansas. During this period he lived apart from his wife and son, seeing them only while on leave, but his devotion to military duties and to a new project of authorship occupied him to the full. On January 1, 1881, Dodge was simultaneously promoted to the rank of colonel and appointed an aide-de-camp to General Sherman, distinctions that bespoke the recognized value of his services under Pope.[71] From 1882 until his retirement from the army in 1891, he commanded the Eleventh Regiment of Infantry, for the first four years at Fort Sully,

70. For a summary of the critical reception of Dodge's book in England and the United States, see "Introduction," in *PNA*, pp. 26–30.

71. See Pope to Dodge, Fort Leavenworth, November 2, 1880; Pope to Dodge (telegram), Fort Leavenworth, December 6, 1880; S.O. 276, Headquarters Department of the Missouri, December 16, 1880; S.O. 283, Headquarters Department of the Missouri, December 24, 1880 (all in Dodge Papers).

Dakota Territory, and thereafter at Madison Barracks, New York. He died in 1895.

In the twentieth century Colonel Dodge has been better remembered for the books and pamphlets he wrote, all outgrowths of his military service, than for that service itself. His place in the Great Sioux War was, after all, only peripheral. The stint as commander of the army escort to the Black Hills Expedition occurred in the months that preceded the outbreak of general hostilities, and the assignment to the Powder River Expedition came as the war was nearing its end. Moreover, the Dull Knife battle, the centerpiece of the latter campaign, was "Mackenzie's Last Fight," as Bourke entitled his narrative—not Dodge's.

Because he possessed a wise awareness of his finitude and also a sense of irony, Dodge would likely smile at the idea that his chief claim to remembrance as an officer in the Powder River Expedition should be his journals, set down in the intervals of leisure during that experience. Yet, owing to his commander's strategy and to the whims of fortune, he had occupied an almost paradoxical position in the campaign, as both a major participant and also something of an onlooker. That double point of view manifests itself often in the journals, some of whose entries reflect his intense engagement with the matters they treat, while others are more detached, discursive, even playful. The sometimes trenchant commentary on Crook and the unfolding campaign is diversified by descriptions of day-to-day events, atmospheric phenomena, anecdotes, characterizations, personal reflections, recollections, and speculations on many topics. Setting down his observations in all their variety was clearly a source of satisfaction to Dodge. His private record of "this most disagreeable winter campaign" is thus an engaging personal document as well as a valuable historical resource.[72] Although Dodge was not present at the celebrated

72. Journal Three, January 3, 1877.

Dull Knife battle, he recorded memorably the efforts of the infantry to join it. Although he did not share Bourke's close contact with General Crook and so possessed less information on some topics than his younger colleague, his wide experience and independent viewpoint were perhaps of yet greater value to him as a contributor to the historical record. Altogether, the journals of Colonel Dodge are the fullest, the most thoughtful, and the most entertaining firsthand account we have of an important U.S. military campaign, the Powder River Expedition of 1876.

Note on Editorial Policy

IN PRESENTING THIS EDITED TEXT OF DODGE'S manuscript journals of the Powder River Expedition, I have tried in general to coordinate realization of two not always compatible goals: fidelity to what the author actually wrote and utility for the reader. Dodge compiled his journals under a variety of circumstances: indoors and outdoors, at leisure and in haste, in comfortable conditions and in awkward or trying ones. Not surprisingly, the character of his journal entries varies widely, from considered, relatively finished discourses to disjointed "telegraphic" notes. Yet despite the variations in their style, the manuscript texts all exhibit Dodge's tendency as a journalist to take liberties with the standard practices of written expression. For example, he freely abbreviated words and names, and at some points he almost dispensed with punctuation. At the ends of lines in the manuscripts he seems to have regarded the pause to shift his pen to the line below as serving adequately—for himself at least—as a substitute for whatever punctuation the context might require.

Dodge felt free to adopt practices like these, in part because he was writing for his own eyes alone. Knowing as he did what his abbreviations signified and how his ideas fit together, he could fashion a shorthand style that suited his private purposes, however ragged or cryptic it might seem to others. Of course, the notebooks in which he wrote imposed a constraint that to some degree obliged him to use the compressed style he did. Small enough to be carried in a shirt pocket or other convenient place, even the largest of the four notebooks afforded him a maximum of 4 5/8 inches per writing line, enough for only five or six words in compressed script. Ordinarily Dodge wrote in a much freer, more expansive hand, but to economize the space taken up by his entries, he adopted a relatively cramped handwriting style.

Presenting the texts of Dodge's manuscript journals in printed form necessitates certain adjustments to make them accessible to a modern reader. The procedures I have followed in editing these texts are summarized below.

When Dodge wrote out words and names in full, he ordinarily spelled with a reasonable degree of accuracy, or at least consistency. He did habitually misspell some words, as *vecinity* for *vicinity*, and he often failed to include the apostrophe in contractions (*dont*, *isnt*), but errors like these pose no difficulties of comprehension. Certain other words and names he spelled in more than one way—for example, *tomorw*, *tomorro*, and *tomorrow*—but the reader quickly grows accustomed to these variations. Thus, except to correct errors so serious as potentially to baffle or so odd as likely to distract, I have allowed Dodge's variant spellings and even misspellings to stand. If confusion seems possible, it is obviated either by an editorial interpolation within square brackets or by a footnote. For proper names that Dodge spells in more than one way, the correct spelling is indicated in an identifying note at the point where that name is first mentioned.

Abbreviations employed by Dodge appear here, with few exceptions, just as he wrote them. Many of these pertain to military matters—*Qr Mr* for *quartermaster*, *Co* or *Compy* for *company*—and quickly become familiar. Others relate to aspects of the weather or else to Dodge's itinerary and location—*ther* or *therm* for *thermometer*, or *m*, *mi*, or *ms* for *miles*—and seem natural enough in their contexts. Abbreviations that may be problematical are filled out within square brackets or explained in notes at the points where they appear. Superscript letters written in connection with abbreviations are brought down to the line except in datelines, for which a standard format is used. When Dodge underscored or otherwise punctuated superscripts, as D^{r}, $D^{r:}$, *or* $D^{r\text{-}}$, the abbreviation is followed here by a period (*Dr.*). When an abbreviation goes unpunctuated, it is given as written (e.g., *Dr*). Ampersands and *&c* (for *et cetera*) are allowed to stand.

Dodge's habits of capitalization, generally conventional though far from consistent, are respected. He did adopt quite often the traditional practice of capitalizing for emphasis, but his intention in doing so is clear and presents no difficulty. Transcribing his entries does involve some uncertainty in distinguishing between capital and lower-case letters. In particular, the letters *C, M,* and *P* create problems of interpretation when they appear at the beginnings of words and especially at the beginnings of lines, for they often rise above the lower-case letters that surround them. In deciding whether to transcribe a letter as capital or lower case, I have taken into consideration both Dodge's habitual practices and also those observable in the immediate context. No effort is made to regularize his capitalization, except that the first letter in proper names and in daily entries is always capitalized.

The inconsistent punctuation and formatting of Dodge's journal entries requires some editorial regularization, for to present it unchanged would result in frequent ambiguity and pervasive distraction. Thus, for example, the sometimes irregular spacing between his paragraphs and entries is regularized unless it seems to carry a special significance, such as to mark a place for information he expected to receive in the future, or to signify text written at a new sitting. Within paragraphs, lines left unfilled toward the right margin are ignored when the spaces have no apparent significance. Similarly, wider than usual spaces between words and between statements are regularized, unless a reason for the practice is discernible.

Dodge habitually observed only slight indentations for the first line of paragraphs; in these journals, with their limited writing space, he indented hardly at all. The problem of determining with confidence whether a small indentation at the left margin was intended to signal a paragraph break or was merely a chance occurrence is often unsolvable. For this reason, paragraph breaks appear in this edited text only when physical evidence, or a combination of physical and contextual evidence, in the manuscript warrants them. When Dodge significantly indents any statement that begins a new line, the line is represented here as the beginning of a paragraph, whether or not its content represents a break in subject matter from the material that has gone before. But when the indentation is even smaller than normal, the new line is considered to begin a paragraph only if the context justifies it. The sole exception to this rule is that throughout the edited journals, each entry that follows a dateline is indented on a new line.

Dodge's terminal punctuation, when he supplied it, took a wide range of forms, from a neat period to a dot extended slightly to the right and perhaps marking a moment of thought, to a yet longer hyphen, and finally to dashes of varying length. The spaces intervening between the final words of statements and these marks of punctuation also varied. To reproduce all the conformations in print is manifestly impossible. Instead, a few rules of thumb are adopted to govern the representation of Dodge's terminal punctuation. If a sentence at the end of a paragraph or a day's entry concludes without a punctuation mark, none is supplied. If, within paragraphs, a sentence concludes without punctuation and the one that follows it begins with a capital letter, no punctuation is supplied. If a sentence concludes with a period or an "extended period," both of which Dodge often (though not always) placed along the line and immediately following the final letter, a period is shown. If a sentence concludes with some longer mark—a hyphen, a dash, or an extended dash—Dodge ordinarily (though not always) placed the punctuation above or else below the line and separated it from the preceding letter by a blank space. Marks like these are shown with one letter-space intervening after the final letter; they appear as en dashes, em dashes, or longer dashes that approximate what Dodge wrote. If, as occasionally occurs, a sentence concludes with a comma, semicolon, or colon, the error is corrected and the change noted. Question marks and exclamation marks are supplied as called for when Dodge concluded sentences without punctuation, but otherwise, his terminal pointing is left essentially as he wrote it.

Dodge liked to record colorful and characteristic dialogue, but in doing so he often failed to complete pairs of quotation marks or did not insert them at all. Thus, when necessary, omitted quotation marks are supplied within brackets. Parentheses and dashes, whether single or in pairs, are treated similarly.

Within sentences, distinguishing between what Dodge may have regarded as commas, hyphens, or something else can be quite difficult. He did write real commas, but these stand at one end of a spectrum of usage. At the other end is a characteristic hyphen or "extended dot," marking both conclusion of a phrase and also, apparently, a moment of thought about what should come next. This latter mark may be arced or slanted upward or downward and may appear above, at, or below the line, but ordinarily a space intervenes between it and whatever precedes it. The variations between these two extremes of internal punctuation are myriad. Although at some points a down-slanted extended dot seems clearly intended by Dodge as a comma, at others the configuration is different enough that such an identification cannot be made with confidence. Fortunately, once one recognizes the effective interchangeability within sentences of Dodge's commas and "extended dots"—or whatever we may call them—problems of interpreting his meaning are rare. In transcribing the journals, I have recorded as hyphens only those marks that clearly justify the identification; they appear in the edited text with a space intervening between them and what precedes them. In more doubtful situations I have interpreted the marks as commas.

Cancellations are relatively infrequent in Dodge's journals, and on the whole they are not especially significant. Most often he deleted matter not to censor himself but to correct errors, insert afterthoughts, and revise for style. However, in the interest of completeness all canceled matter is included here, except that deleted words and phrases that he immediately rewrote are ignored. Mere slips of the pencil and canceled fragments of illegible letters are also ignored.

Dodge often employed the caret (^) to indicate placement of inserted matter. Here the caret is used to denote interlineated material, which is shown in a free space above the printed line (see the list of editorial symbols and abbreviations below). In the few instances where he inserted an asterisk or other mark to show the proper placement of material located elsewhere, the situation is explained in a note.

Dodge assigned no page numbers in any of his journals. Ordinarily he wrote his entries straightforwardly, more or less filling each page, writing first on the front and then on the back of each leaf, and passing from front to back in a journal. No systematic numbering of pages is supplied here, but to facilitate the location of drawings, blank pages, reversed text, and other variations from the norm, page numbers are shown within square brackets at the points where that information is called for. The page numbers given are designated *R* for *recto*, the first or front side of a sheet on which Dodge ordinarily wrote before turning it over, or else *V* for *verso*, the reverse side. Thus *[38V]* means the reverse side of the thirty-eighth manuscript page. Page-numbers given without *R* or *V* denote both sides of a sheet.

Dodge's drawings in the journals are all maps of the country he was then traversing. Although they are not reproduced here, their presence and chief features are noted at the points where they appear.

Dodge began almost all his entries with a dateline, but in doing so he adopted several formats, providing varying amounts of information. On some occasions he recorded the day of the week, the date, the month, the year, and the location; at other times he set down something much briefer. Often he drew a line or a row of hatchmarks across the page to separate the dateline from the entry that followed; at other times he began the entry immediately to the right of the date. When he added a place name or a camp number, as he often did while compiling an itinerary to be reported later, he might write it at the beginning or the end of his dateline, or else above or below it.

Some consistency is imposed here on these diverse practices. Making use of all the information Dodge included in any particular dateline, but presenting at a minimum the month and date, the information is given in the following format:

> *Designation of day (e.g., Thanksgiving), day of the week, month, date, year. Place, camp number*

Abbreviations in the manuscript dateline, as *March 23*rd, are deleted, so that in this case the date would appear as *March 23*.

EDITORIAL SYMBOLS AND ABBREVIATIONS

[roman] Editorial additions

[*italic*] Editorial explanations

< > Restorations of canceled matter. Cancellations immediately written over are shown next to the letters or numerals written over them, without intervening space.

[? ?] or [?] Doubtful readings. The question marks are used within square or angle brackets. A single doubtful word is followed immediately by a question mark within square brackets, without an intervening space.

unrecovered	Unrecovered word. When more than one word is involved, the fact is indicated (e.g., "*three words unrecovered*").
∧	Interlinear insertions

Editorial situations not covered by these symbols are explained in the notes.

The Powder River Expedition Journals of Colonel Richard Irving Dodge

Journal One: October 31–December 1, 1876

October 31, 1876. Omaha Barracks, Nebraska[1]

On the 29th of Oct, & when returning from a trip to Fort Fetterman,[2] I met on the cars Col Royall of the 3d Cavy, just from the front.[3] He informed me that I would, in all probability be detailed to com[man]d the Infantry in Crooks Winter Expedition. Genl Merritt[4] & others gave me the same information. I am executor of an estate <not> but have not yet had the will proved.[5] It was very necessary for others, that the will

1. This manuscript journal consists of sixty-nine unnumbered pages in a copy of "Office Scratch Book No. 3," a cardboard pad measuring 4 13/16 x 7 7/16 inches, to which are attached sheets of plain unlined paper measuring 4 5/8 x 6 1/2 inches. Five sheets, not numbered here, have been torn away at the front, leaving only stubs. The text on the first three remaining leaves indicates that the notebook had served Dodge during the Black Hills Expedition of 1875. It includes no identifying marks other than a conspicuous encircled "1" on the first surviving page, [1R]. The text is written entirely in pencil. Pages [1]–[3] contain a miscellany of jottings and maps, all relating to the Black Hills Expedition; pp. [2V] and [3V] are blank. The text begins on p. [4R].

2. Dodge had been at Fort Fetterman on court-martial duty between October 19 and October 27.

3. Lieutenant Colonel William B. Royall, Third Cavalry, had commanded a battalion under General George Crook during the summer campaign. He had reached Fort Laramie on October 26 and when Dodge met him was bound for Omaha to begin service as inspector general for the Department of the Platte.

4. Colonel Wesley Merritt, Fifth Cavalry, whom Dodge refers to by his brevet rank, had commanded a battalion in the Big Horn and Yellowstone expedition under General Crook. At the dissolution of that command his regimental headquarters had been relocated to Fort D. A. Russell, near Cheyenne.

5. Dodge's mother-in-law, Maria Paulding, had died at Omaha Barracks on August 5, 1876.

be proved at once. It was barely possible that I could get through this business in time to attend to my military duties – I telegraphed to Genl Crook the Dept Com[man]d[e]r <at> (now at Fort Laramie) as follows.

Omaha <Bk> Neb.
Oct 31, 1876.

Genl Geo. Crook
Comdg Dept.
Fort Laramie
Business very important to others requires my presence <at>in New York. If am to go with expedition please give me leave for ten days immediately. If I dont go with expedition leave is not necessary at present.

I waited in Omaha with some anxiety – the result – at 5 p.m. I recd <the> a telegram as follows –

Fort Laramie
Oct 31, 1876 –

Col R I Dodge
Omaha B[arrac]ks –
If you wish to command the Infantry Batallions, in the Expedition, fifteen companies there will not be time to take the leave refused – (requested?)[6] Can you go or not – Answer –

By Comd of Genl Crook
s[i]g[ne]d Nickerson
A. D. C.[7]

A plain offer from which it is impossible for me to back down with credit.

I therefore immediately sent <the> telegram as follows.

6. Apparently the parenthesized word is Dodge's query of an erroneously transcribed telegraph message.

7. Captain Azor H. Nickerson, Twenty-third Infantry, was General Crook's senior aide-de-camp. He was about to return to Omaha after a summer of service in the field.

Omaha Bks, Neb
Oct. 31, 1876

Capt A H Nickerson
A. D. C.
Telegram received – I accept the Command –

Signed R. I. Dodge
Lt. Col. 23 Infy.

Paid visits until 9 pm then wrote to Father enclosing check for $100 for Sis Molly – to Cousin Kate Chambless enclosing $300 check for an investment in real estate & also to Tooty, giving her the news to date ——[8]

November 1, 1876. Omaha Barracks, Nebraska

Went to town 11 am – & directly to HdQrs. Order for me recd at HdQrs.[9] I will get it tomorw. Goodale was going west to join his Co. I stopped him & take him up with me.[10] Did a tremendous lot of work. Saw Manderson,[11] & got a paper or petition declining the executorship of Ma P.'s estate – in favor

8. Dodge's exact relationship to his Cousin Kate, to whom he more than once sent funds, is uncertain. Members of the Chambliss family, including John Randolph Chambliss (1809–75) and his son John, Jr. (1833–64), had incurred heavy debts during the Civil War, in which they took up the Confederate cause. The Chambliss family owned property near Dodge's childhood home in North Carolina. "Tooty" was a nickname for his wife, Julia Rhinelander Paulding Dodge (b. 1837).

9. S.O. 147, U.S. Army, Department of the Platte (hereafter cited as DP), Field Records, Powder River Expedition, dated November 1, 1876, directed Dodge to "proceed to Medicine Bow Station and march with Companies C, G, and I, 23rd Infantry, for Fort Fetterman." Since 1866 the headquarters of the military department had been in the city of Omaha, three miles southeast of Omaha Barracks.

10. First Lieutenant Greenlief A. Goodale, Company K, Twenty-third Infantry, was returning from a leave of absence. His unit had been stationed at Sidney Barracks, Nebraska, but had received orders to take post at Cantonment Reno, Wyoming Territory, the supply depot for the Powder River Expedition. Goodale assumed command of his company at Cantonment Reno on November 20.

11. Charles F. Manderson (1837–1911), who had risen to brigadier general of volunteers in the Union army during the Civil War, had resided in Omaha since 1869 and was prominent in local affairs. Manderson was elected to the U.S. Senate from Nebraska in 1883 and 1889.

of Julia. Bought lots of things – Boots, arctics, gloves, chamois shirts, drawers, &c. Made out pay a/cs[12] for Novr & Decr. & left them with Omaha National Bank for collection.

Gave Byron Reed[13] the policy of insurance on my furniture, with directions to renew after 27th Novr & draw on Bank for amount. A terrible day – snow slush &c. &c. Came home wet through stuck my feet in cold water & put on dry clothing. Took a nap after dinner. At night wrote to Tooty enclosing the paper referred to above – to the Putnams, giving list of persons to whom I want my book sent with authors compliments, to

(J. H.)

Potter ^ and to Earl Dunraven.[14] Expected to start tomorw but the Cos are not ready. Will go the day after tomorro ——

November 2, 1876. Omaha Barracks, Nebraska

Yesterday paid Com[missar]y Bill – Vegetable Man – Lacy Sheely.[15] The day before paid Joe & Laura.[16] Owe nothing

12. Accounts.

13. A longtime resident of Omaha, Byron Reed was president of a real estate agency on Fourteenth Street that also handled conveyancing, loans, and insurance.

14. Owing to delays in transmitting plates and proofsheets from the English publisher, Chatto and Windus of London, the publication in the United States of *The Plains of the Great West and Their Inhabitants*, by G. P. Putnam's Sons of New York, did not occur until January 1877. Dodge's list of recipients for complimentary copies included Colonel Joseph Haydn Potter, Twenty-fifth Infantry, and Windham Thomas Wyndham-Quin (1841–1926), the earl of Dunraven, to each of whom he wrote at this time. In 1875 Dodge had corresponded about the forthcoming book with Colonel Potter, who had been his immediate superior in the Thirtieth Infantry between 1866 and 1869. The earl of Dunraven was a former hunting companion of Dodge, and in July 1876 the two men had formed tentative plans for a fall hunt in the vicinity of Fort Fred Steele, Wyoming Territory (Dodge to William Blackmore, Omaha Barracks, August 2, 1876, Blackmore Papers).

15. John M. Sheely, with his brother Joseph, ran a meat market at 259 Douglas Street, Omaha. He lived outside town on the "Military Road." He or a member of his family was likely the person referred to by Dodge as the "Vegetable Man."

16. Joe and Laura, a husband and wife who resided and sometimes traveled with Dodge, were his valued domestic servants. In his journal entry

Went to Town, ready to go off but Bob W.[17] has heard nothing of Pollock,[18] & advised me to stay. Bought several things needed. Ordered a pair of Mex[ica]n leggins, & paid $9 for a skin (Llama) Wrote to Father & Mother, & to Tooty at night & was so busy I could not visit the Ladies

November 3, 1876. Omaha Barracks

Up early. Gave Joe chks for $50 – dated Novr 30 and Decr 31. Drew all my money out of Bank. Made pay accts for Novr & Decr & left them in Omaha Natl Bank to be drawn when due.

Bade good by to Bob, to Kirk[,] Luddington,[19] &c. & started well-fixed for Med[icine]. Bow. Train late. Goodale with me. Got transp. & sleeping berths from Kirk Start with bad cold

November 4. Medicine Bow

Arrived 12. midnight. All in bed except Dr Ousley.[20] Had pleasant enough journey on cars, but were behind hand all the time. Found very pleasant set of Californians on the cars. Got a good room at Trabings,[21] & went to bed 12.30 am

---

for September 11, 1880, he praised Laura as "an excellent hand always ready for work, not a lazy bone in her body" (Dodge Papers).

17. Lieutenant Colonel Robert Williams was assistant adjutant general for the Department of the Platte.

18. Captain Otis W. Pollock, Company C, Twenty-third Infantry, was post commander at Sidney Barracks, Nebraska. Although he was relieved of the command on November 2, he did not join the Powder River Expedition immediately, owing to a delay in settling accounts at that post.

19. In addition to Colonel Williams, Dodge singles out two staff officers, Captain Ezra B. Kirk and Major Marshall I. Ludington. Major Ludington was assistant quartermaster general for the Department of the Platte.

20. Acting Assistant Surgeon W. T. Owsley, one of six physicians who accompanied the Powder River Expedition.

21. August and Charles Trabing, who ran a business transporting military supplies to Fort Fetterman from this station on the Union Pacific Rail Road, also operated a lodging for travelers stopping at Medicine Bow.

November 5. Camp on Little Medicine Bow

Slept well. Off[icer]s reported before breakfast. Find here Co[mpanie]s C, G & I 23d Infy. Dr. Hoff, Lt. Pease 4th Infy,[22] & 2 Hospl Stewards all wanting transpn. QrMrs Agent informs me that he has only one wagon to Compy. – General row. Snow on ground – blowing like the D—l. Every prospect of a villainous trip & not half transpn enough.

Assumed Comd. Appointed Goodale Adjt & Qr Mr Gave orders to start 11 am – could not load stuff on wagons [–] bullied agent & got more.

After great trouble got off at 12 m – some drunken men of course. Wagons badly loaded – However arrived at Lit Med Bow, 4.30 pm & camped.

Got a wall tent from Carpenter[23] & some mess supplies from Trabing. Dr. Hoff & wife, Dr. Ousley & Goodale messed with me. Soldier cook pretty good. Very cold, blustery & disagreeable day – with some snow. Ride the horses I brought down from Coates for the hunt.[24] No stove, cold night. slept tolerably however Distance 9. miles – no wood or grass

November 6, 1876. Second Crossing, Little Medicine Bow

Pretty good breakfast & got off at 8 a.m. – Rode ahead with Goodale & Dr. Ousley, & tried to get an antelope. Saw plenty at distance & got a long shot, 400 yds at a herd, but missed. Got 3 sage grouse with rifle. Saw several hundred, & might have bagged many. Day cold & windy but clear. Marching *hard*

22. Assistant Surgeon John V. R. Hoff and First Lieutenant William B. Pease, the latter of the Ninth (not Fourth) Infantry, were both on their way to Fort Fetterman to join the Powder River Expedition. Dr. Hoff, who was traveling with his wife, had also been assigned to Fort Fetterman as post surgeon. He reached the fort on November 8.

23. Captain Gilbert S. Carpenter, Fourteenth Infantry, with whom Dodge had recently served together at a court-martial at Fort Fetterman.

24. Captain Edwin M. Coates, Fourth Infantry, was post commander at Fort Fetterman through November 15 of this year. By "the hunt" Dodge probably means an excursion made on the return to Medicine Bow after his recent stay at the fort.

on green troops & many stragglers. Went into camp 2.30 p.m. – all in by 3.30. Weather moderated – pleasant evening – Distance 18 miles – no wood or grass –

November 7, 1876. Near Cabin Creek, Box Elder Canon

Broke camp 8 a.m. Slept well. No wind – but very cold towards morning. Lovely day. Comd started well, & by 11.30 reached the last crossing of the Little Med Bow, 10 miles.

Left there at 12, & at 3.30 <c>made camp on Box Elder, half a mile below Cabin. Road fine no snow in canon. Men are however very soft, & there were many stragglers. Will not try to go in in two days as intended Bagged a fine antelope today, & had part for supper as did all the offs. Good camp. Fair grass wood & water good & abundant Distance 20 miles[25]

November 8, 1876. Near Dug out, Box Elder Canon

Night warm considering altitude which must be over 8000 feet above level of sea. Slept tolerably, but waked up very often, & as often wished for morning. I think one needs less sleep in these very high altitudes. Another curious result of the rarified atmosphere is the swelling of my feet. I noticed this when I was here before. I am wearing an old pair of riding boots made for me in Feby '63 & which I have worn ever since to Arizona, through the Black Hills, & on all my hunts & rides since – never finding them uncomfortable – but always being able to put them on easily even when wet. Here they have gone back on me. I get them on with the greatest difficulty & they bind (without hurting) all day – At Ft Fetterman on the Ct Martial I could not get them on at all, & had to sit on the Court in slippers – All my leather boots & shoes are in the same fix – so I shall I fear be reduced to cloth. The camp of

25. Dodge added the notation of distance in a penciled box at the upper left on p. [10R].

last night was fairly good but contracted. Wagons & men too close for comfort, & the noises of the mules kept me awake –

Got off in good time a little before 8. oclk. Dr Hoff & wife left us to make the trip to Ft Fetterman today. Weather perfectly beautiful & so warm that I fear it is a "weather breeder." Determined to march only to end of canon, as that is the last camping place unless I make more than 2<8>3 miles. I reached the campg place at 11 am. The Comd an hour later, officers & men pretty stiff & sore. Have a very good camp – plenty of wood & water – grass as good as can be found at this season – Scenery fine very wild & picturesque. We leave the Box Elder tomorw & go on the Divide between it & La Prele

Distance today <8>10 miles –

November 9, 1876. 12 Mile Spring

Had a most luxurious bath last evening, a rare luxury when campg out, & rigged myself with clean clothing from head to foot. The night was very cold towards a.m., & I needed all the covers I had. Got off at 7.30 a.m. to make as we supposed a long march. Was not long at all. I arrived at camping place at 11.30, & the Command came in in good order at about 1 pm.

Met Dewees & wife, O'Brien & wife & 2d Lt & wife same Compy, all going to join Co at Ft Sanders – also Ferris going to Med Bow on a frolic[?][26] & Mrs Dr [*blank*] leaving her husband who goes with me. Dewees says that we are to have many comforts that other exp[editio]ns did not have – Am glad of it.[27] Wrote to Tooty & Dad last night & sent the letters by the mail man whom we met today. Had a very pleasant

26. Captain Thomas B. Dewees, Company A, Second Cavalry, and First Lieutenant Martin E. O'Brien, also of Company A, Second Cavalry. The other lieutenant of that company was Second Lieutenant Daniel C. Pearson. These persons, with Captain Samuel P. Ferris, Fourth Infantry, had all participated in the summer campaign.

27. The overshoes, sealskin caps and gloves, and woolen mittens provided for the troops of the Powder River Expedition are described in McChristian, *The U.S. Army in the West, 1870–1880*, pp. 174–77.

evening, the weather permitting enjoyment of tents without fire. We have come down 2000 feet at least today I am to be a Brig[adier]. Gen[eral] on the expn with several Batallions.[28] No game. Dr Hoff sent us some bread – most exceptable. Sent in my worst sick men – by wagon Splendid day, tho' warm – Excellent marching. Distance 15 miles – Good water wood & grass ——

November 10, 1876. Fort Fetterman

Broke Camp at 7.30 am reached this post at 11 am Command arrived an hour or two later. Reported at once to Genl. Crook, & was given my Comd. Met Townsend & Campbell.[29] Am in doubt about the organization of my Comd. The presence of a Field Offr & the necessity of allowing him his Comd forces on me the necessity of playing Brig Genl. I prefer to have direct comd but cant help myself.

Gave all the Infy to Townsend & all the Arty to Campbell. Have got started nicely. Went up in afternoon, & saw the Genl. Had a long talk with him after dinner. He is very liberal in his allowances, & says laughingly that he wishes he had taken my advice last year as to his Indian Campaigns.[30] Dined at

28. That is, he was to command a brigade—a group of regiments, or in this case battalions, combined into a single body. The Powder River Expedition consisted of two brigades, one of cavalry under Colonel Ranald S. Mackenzie, Fourth Cavalry, the other of artillery and infantry under Dodge. The artillery battalion comprised Batteries C, F, H, and K, Fourth Artillery. The infantry component included Companies A, B, D, F, I, and K, Ninth Infantry; Companies D and G, Fourteenth Infantry; and Companies C, G, and I, Twenty-third Infantry (G.O. 1, November 10, 1876, HQIAB).

29. Major Edwin F. Townsend, Ninth Infantry, who had just been relieved as post commander at Fort Laramie, and Captain Joseph B. Campbell, Fourth Artillery. Townsend, who was promoted to lieutenant colonel in 1879, served under Dodge with the Eleventh Infantry from 1882 until his promotion to colonel in 1886. In the sentences that follow Dodge describes the chain of command, which placed him below the "field officer" in the Powder River Expedition, General Crook, and over the two brigades commanded by Townsend and Campbell.

30. Dodge had advocated increased reliance upon infantry in campaigns against Indians. For a fuller account of Dodge's earlier conversation with Crook, see Journal Four.

mess. Saw lots of offs some old acquaintances but most<ly> new – played Billiards in evening, & came to camp late with Campbell & Smith Arty[31] – all feeling very well.

November 11, 1876. Fort Fetterman

Remained in camp all day to sign papers & got the comd properly set up. Very hard matter to get the Maj. Infy to do anything energetically. <D>However there is no use in being troubled. Went up to camp about 4 pm Saw the Genl, attended to business. Dined at the mess. Played billiards – & came home with Goodale about 12 p.m.

Very bad political news from the States. Looks like a row.[32]

November 12, 1876. Fort Fetterman

Went up to post pretty early this morning – through a real plains snow storm. I expected to cross the river today, but reported to the Genl that a move in the snow would result in sickness. He delayed the march & we do not now know when we will get off – Got boots, socks Com[missar]y stores, & some articles from store. All are very polite and good natured, but the Post QrMr is an awfully slow cuss – too handsome to be of much account.[33] Nearly all our wants are supplied today

31. Captain Frank G. Smith, Fourth Artillery.

32. The fiercely contested presidential campaign of 1876 had culminated in an election whose results remained in doubt throughout the period covered by these journals. Adherents of both Rutherford B. Hayes, the Republican candidate, and Samuel Tilden, his Democratic opponent, claimed victory in the pivotal states—North Carolina, South Carolina, Louisiana, and Florida—but nothing definite could be established until the official counts were complete. Accusations of irregularities at the polls aggravated the tense situation, and in Florida the rival parties actually threatened bloodshed. Anticipating an outbreak of civil violence, Brigadier General Christopher C. Augur dispatched military forces to the danger areas. Rutherford B. Hayes was declared president-elect by a joint session of Congress on March 2, 1877. In the interval the potential for armed conflict was taken seriously.

33. The post quartermaster at Fort Fetterman was First Lieutenant George O. Webster, Fourth Infantry. On November 23 his duties were assumed by First Lieutenant John W. Bubb of the same regiment.

& this Comd will be ready to march by tomorw noon – not that I expect or want to go then.

The sun set clear, & it is now 10 pm, as cold as Christmas. A days sun will clear off the snow – & we may expect to get away on Tuesday. Failed to get my tent today, & consequently am sitting[?] out Goodale & the Dr. No stove in my present tent. Coates promises to have me fixed by 10 am tomorw – Distributed the horses – Clark is doing very well as aaqm.[34] Wrote long letter to Tooty tonight. Goodale just finishing the 37th page of a letter to his wife, & the Dr. fast asleep

November 13, 1876. Fort Fetterman

Heavy fog & mist this a.m. but the sun finally came out bright & clear. The cold last night was intense – 13° below zero at 8 am. Sent circular to Compy Comdrs to report wants All reported all ready –

Coates gave me a splendid tent, & for the first time on this march I am comfortable in my own tent – Got a tressle for my bed, 4 camp stools, 2 tables – Coates gave me a leather backed chair. Went up & reported all right to Genl – invited to lunch – Had pleasant time. Paid Comy bill – wash bill – 2 dinners at mess – settled with suttler[35] – got pair of buffalo shoes. Got orders to leave tomorw. River half frozen & crossing execrable. Returned to Camp 2 pm – Issued order of march – & got all ready for tomorw. Rumor in camp that McKenzie is set to march tomorw – Glad of it – Coates visited me at night. Wrote letters to Tooty Dad & Kate Chambless – Changed my underclothing & got ready for work –

34. First Lieutenant William L. Clarke, Twenty-third Infantry, was acting assistant quartermaster for the artillery and infantry battalions. Dodge invariably spells his surname "Clark."

35. Between 1871 and 1880 the sutler, or post trader, at Fort Fetterman was E. Tillotson.

November 14, 1876. Sage Creek, Ten Miles from Fort Fetterman

Had a splendid nights rest in my new bed – which I have gotten after much tribulation. It is only a pair of low tressles and 3 boards, but they keep me off the cold ground & make no end of difference in my comfort. The stove too is first rate. Reveille was only too early this morning. Got up however & roused the lazy ones – Dr. Ousley got his ankle sprained last night & is quite a cripple.

The river is my terror. Made arrangements so that no soldiers would have to wade, but this made my start necessarily very late. Sent each companies wagon half loaded to the river with half the compy. These men mounted on it, were carried across, unloaded the wagon <&> which was then sent back empty for the other property & men. The Platte River is here only about 50 yards wide, but it is very swift, & generally too deep to ford. There are however several good fords near the post, but as the river was full of floating ice & the banks lined with ice several inches thick, I anticipated great difficulty in crossing. Fury's (Qr *master*)[36] Wagon Camp was fortunately on the other side & the constant passage of wagons & teams had kept one ford quite open. To my very great gratification I found but little trouble, beyond the delay & had every thing over by 10.30 am. Went up to HdQrs – saw the General who gave me carte blanche as to camping – posted my letters – bade good by to Coates & returned to my Comd. Just at 11.30 all being ready I gave orders for the march.

McKenzie had crossed at a ford some two miles above & having no fears of wetting the feet of his cavalrymen, he had got a good start of me.[37] The pack train crossed at same ford as

36. Captain John V. Furey was chief quartermaster of the Powder River Expedition. In view of Dodge's later criticism of Furey, the underlined "master" at this point is likely ironic.

37. The cavalry under Colonel Mackenzie consisted of Company K, Second Cavalry; Companies H and K, Third Cavalry; Companies B, D, E, F, I, and M of the Fourth Cavalry (Mackenzie's regiment); and Companies H and L, Fifth Cavalry.

Powder River Expedition crossing the North Platte River, November 14, 1876 (*Harper's Weekly*, December 16, 1876)

McKenzie & were also ahead. Behind us came Egan & his Company of Grays – the Hd Qr Guard. The Pawnees under Major North came after –[38] It was a beautiful & exhilerating sight, the long lines of Cavalry Artillery Infantry Indians pack mules & wagons. The ground was covered with snow, but the day was perfectly lovely – too warm indeed for good marching. The snow was in many places too deep & wet for the Infantry to keep in <in> – while the road was muddy & slippery from the passage of so many animals & wagons. However the Doboys got along excellently, slow but sure, & at 3.10 arrived at our camping place on Sage Creek. It is only a creek in a rainy season – being now a series of water holes containing a scant supply of poor water. McKenzie went to the head, & I took the holes lowest down. The Comd is now extended for three miles along the valley – & makes a brave show. I have never seen so large and well fitted a Comd in Indian warfare –

I do not think I have enumerated our forces heretofore. McKenzie has 13 companies of Cavalry – divided into three battalions. I have 4 Comps of Artillery & 11 Comps of Infy – divided into two battalions. There are about 100 Pawnee Indians under Maj North, about 60 Arrapahoes under Lieut. [*blank*] about 100 Sioux under [*blank*][39] Our <wagon> train

38. Captain James Egan's Company K, Second Cavalry, had served ably with General Crook's Big Horn Expedition in the spring of this year. See Hedren, *Fort Laramie in 1876*, pp. 68–70; Robinson, *A Good Year to Die*, pp. 76–80. A detachment of Pawnee scouts, under Major Frank North and his brother Luther, had journeyed north from the Indian Territory to join the Powder River Expedition. The military service of the Pawnees under the Norths is detailed in Grinnell, *Two Great Scouts and Their Pawnee Battalion*. See also Hyde, *The Pawnee Indians*, pp. 336–39; and Danker, ed., *Man of the Plains*, pp. 205–25.

39. The Indian scouts, whom John G. Bourke characterized in *Mackenzie's Last Fight with the Cheyennes*, p. 5, as "a superb lot of men, physically and mentally," numbered at this time 363. They included 91 Shoshones and 15 Bannocks, under Tom Cosgrove, "Texas Bob" Eckles, and First Lieutenant Walter S. Schuyler, Fifth Cavalry; 100 Pawnees under the North brothers; and 155 Arapahoes, Cheyennes, and Sioux from Red Cloud Agency, under First

consists of 300 wagons, 8 ambulances, & 300 pack mules.[40] We have 30 days subsistence & forage for nearly that time – Each Company has 200 rounds of ammunition per man, & the supply train carries at least 300 more. Egan with his Compy of 2d Cavy is Genl Crooks Hd Qr Guard. We will find 30 days rations & forage at Fort Reno, in case we get short –

Genl Crook came into camp just after I got my tent pitched, but soon left for his own camp about a quarter of a mile above me. He is in first rate spirits – & has a right to be – I am camped at what is called the 12 mile camp on Sage Creek. The distance is really but little over 8 miles from Ft Fetterman, but all distances on the frontier are long when estimated by contractors who are paid by the 100 miles. When it comes to be measured the 85 miles from Fetterman to Reno will likely dwindle to 70 – Delightful day. Poor camp. We brought wood – as this creek offers nothing but poor water – no grass Have done a splendid days work & we start under good auspices.

November 15, 1876. Camp on South Cheyenne

Broke camp at 7.15 am. Soon passed the supply train but everything else being already ahead beat us into camp. The day was blustery & felt like snow, but was not uncomfortable. Road good & the snow nearly all evaporated by the warm wind of last night

Troops marched excellently, & got into camp 2.30. The whole Comd is camped on this stream which is a miserable branch that can be stepped over anywhere. The pack mules

---

Lieutenant William Philo Clark, Second Cavalry. One company of Sioux was commanded by Second Lieutenant Hayden De Lany, Ninth Infantry. The scouts also included one Ute and one Nez Percé.

40. In his diary entry for November 9, Bourke described the transportation in detail as including a train of 168 wagons and ambulances, with 219 drivers and attendants, all civilian personnel. The 400 mules were maintained by 65 expert packers (Bourke Papers).

have the camp I designed for my Comd, and I was forced to take a sandy & rather contracted position on the south side of the *River.* The road today has been monotonous in the extreme – except that when we got on the high divide between the waters of the Platte & Cheyenne, we had a magnificent view of the Laramie Range of mountains the same that we came through in coming from Medicine Bow.

Water at Browns Spring 3 miles from here. This is a good camp tho' the grass is poor – *plenty* of wood & water – Distance about 18 miles – called 22 –

Went up to Genl Crooks Camp in evening, hoping to see McKenzie whom I have not yet met on the campaign. He had been there but was gone. Played 5 games of whist against Genl Crook, I having Fury as partner – he Clark – Beat them 3 of the 5 – Very dark & threatening rain – Gave orders for very early start tomorw, hoping to beat some of these people into camp.

All getting on splendidly – quite warm tonight but looks threatening.

November 16, 1876. Camp on Wind Creek

Reveille at 5.15 – broke camp 6.30. Moved to this early effort because Genl Crook gives his Indians & pack mules the very best camps if they are ahead. Early as I was however McKenzie got ahead on the road with his wagons, I (from the peculiarly mean position assigned me last night) having to make over a mile of deep sand before I struck the road. Fury came up & regulated us by putting Hdqr trains ahead. Genl Crook passes for a Sybarite – who utterly contemns anything like luxury or even comfort[41] – yet he has the most luxurious surroundings, considering the necessity for short allowance that I have ever seen taken to the field by a Genl Officer –

41. Dodge means the opposite of what he writes, for a sybarite is one devoted to luxury and pleasure.

There is no doubt of his courage, energy <or> will – but I am loath to say I begin to believe he is a humbug – who hopes to make reputation by assuming qualities foreign to him.[42] One thing is most certain. He is the very worst mannered man I have ever seen in his position. Though his ill manners seem to be the result rather of ignorance than of deliberate will – I believe him to be warm hearted – but his estimate of a man will I think be discovered to be founded not on what that man can or will do for the Service, but what he can or will do for Crook. It speaks badly for mankind when I am obliged to
that kind
admit, that <those> ^ are the successful men —

The day has been lovely. The slight shower of last night laid the dust & made marching good. Though McKenzie got his wagons first on the road, I was a long way ahead of him with my troops & he was forced into all kinds of bad ground with his command. I got to the camping place an hour ahead of my comd. Went to Genl C. to see where I should camp, & was turned off to hunt for myself – all the choice spots being appropriated by him, his Indians & pack mules. These two last are his hobbies & he rides them all the time.[43] All the Hd Qr

42. Dodge's doubt about the genuineness of Crook's ostensible distaste for luxurious living while in the field indicates his awareness of an article, "General Crook's Sham Simplicity of Life," that appeared in the *New York Herald*, October 2, 1876. Here Reuben B. Davenport, who had accompanied Crook's command during the summer, accused the general of playing a double game: leading a life of spartan simplicity when in public view, then behaving as "a consistent mirror of selfishness" when surrounded in private by his "familiars and toadies" (p. 2). Dodge mentions Davenport by name later in this entry; and see the introduction, p. 16. While at Red Cloud Agency in late October Crook categorically denied to another interviewer the allegations by the *New York Herald* correspondent. See the *Chicago Tribune*, November 14, 1876, p. 4.

43. In contrast to other military leaders, including his immediate superior General Sheridan, Crook regarded Indian auxiliaries as reasonably amenable to discipline, trustworthy, and capable of providing valuable information that could be obtained through no other means. At the close of the summer campaign he explained to Cuthbert Mills of the *New York Times* that he always sought the assistance of Indian scouts "because scouting with them is

animals, the pack mules & the mules of the supply trains are above us – while his Indians wash the entrals of the beeves in the stream from which his troops have to drink below — The Cavy & Infy are nobodies. The Indians & pack mules have all the good places. He scarcely treats McKenzie & I decently, but he will spend hours chatting pleasantly with an Indian, or a dirty scout – I don't blame Davenport of the Herald one bit. He stated what he saw & is cordially hated for it. I cant state what I see except in this private journal

My troops arrived in camp at 2 pm The road is abominable up and down all the time, with very steep pitches, making it hard for men & animals. Maj Stanton[44] arrived tonight with an immense mail, but nothing for me. Not a single letter from any of my loved ones, & I am sorely disappointed. It makes one feel <very> all alone in the world to see every one around him devouring letters from their loved [ones] & their friends, when no letter comes to him –

Went over at night to see McKenzie. He was most gentlemanly & agreeable, & I enjoyed my visit. He gave me two orderlies – & asked me to call on him for any thing I want, & he would help me if he could. The news now is that Hayes is elected – good news to all of us who wish to hold our positions as army officers.[45] Had several calls after my return from the Cavy Camp, & spent a pleasant evening. McKenzie &

---

the business of their lives. They learn all the signs of a trail as a child learns the alphabet; it becomes an instinct. . . . They would be of immense use" ("The Indian Campaign," October 11, 1876, p. 5). For Crook's ideas about the value of pack mule transportation in campaigns against Indians, see the introduction, pp. 18, 33–34.

44. Major Thaddeus H. Stanton, the paymaster, was chief of scouts for the Department of the Platte and his commander's trusted troubleshooter.

45. The Democratic platform in the presidential campaign of 1876 had advocated "army reform," a euphemism for reduction in forces. A full-page cartoon satirizing the folly of the Democrats in proposing to weaken the already small army during a time of Indian conflict appeared in *Harper's Weekly*, 20, no. 1022 (July 29, 1876), 609.

I agreed not to struggle for the road. He is to have it one day, I the next. Distance today 18 miles – Road bad – fair camp – No wood – but good water & some grass. Several streams today – Middle Cheyenne 8 miles, Humphreyville 12 miles, North Cheyenne 17 miles, Wind Creek 18 miles.

November 17, 1876.
Dry Fork of Powder River, Camp at Buffalo Springs

Reveille at 5 am. & got comd off at 6.10. It looked threatening & a little rain fell while we were getting our breakfast, but as it was my morning for starting early I pushed things. Before my wagons had started it commenced to snow. I called for my wraps & furs & had almost to unload the wagons before they were found. By this time it was snowing furiously, & when I at last mounted my horse it was with the greatest difficulty that I could make him face the gale – For about an hour we had as lively a snow storm, as I have seen. My Ku Klux Cap[46] is very comfortable except that the eyes are not protected, & the little hard pellets of snow striking the eyeballs were painful & tended to keep a man down cast. My men bore it bravely, though as the storm struck us after we broke camp many of them were without overcoats, & <nearly> scarcely any had face protection – They plodded along, wind dead ahead, blowing hard. Cold as Christmas – without anything but their own stout hearts to protect them, & on a little let-up of the storm some glorious fellow struck up "We are marching on" –[47] At least a hundred voices joined in at once & though I was riding on the side of the Column, <&> have no more voice than a crow, & moreover have the dignity of Acting Brigadier General to support, I could hardly refrain from striking in –

46. That is, a hood covering the entire head and neck except the eyes, similar in style to one forming part of Ku Klux Klan regalia. Dodge was not a member of the Klan.

47. In *Our Wild Indians* Dodge identified this song, struck up by the "sweet but manly voice" of "some glorious fellow in the ranks," as "Marching through Georgia" (p. 509).

It is a glorious life this soldiering. However great the trials discomforts or suffering there is pluck endurance & patience to counterbalance all – We are going on a campaign fraught with not only the natural dangers from the enemy, but with a thousand unnamed dangers from the elements. Yet not a man flinches – not one but would rather suffer all than turn back – A better Comd than this never fell to the lot of a Commander & if Crook dont do something with it, he is a very unlucky, or incapable man – After about two hours march the storm passed, & with a flurry or two, left us entirely though the weather turned so cold that our extra snow wraps were very comfortable –

The day finally cleared and after 12 m was as pleasant as could be desired – I reached camp 1 p.m. The Comd got in at 2.10 – after an 8 hours march Called on Stanton Paymaster at Genl C's Hd Qrs. He is very busy making up pay rolls, so I did not disturb him except for a moment. McKenzie came over to my tent after & we had a long talk.

Four Snake Indians joined us tonight with information that the hostiles are moving to the other side of the Big Horn Mts.[48] So we are likely to have a Mountain rather than a Plains Campaign, to my very great satisfaction.

20 Miles today – very little water – otherwise a good camp.

A body of 8 Indians supposed to be hostiles were seen watching the column from a distance. 15 Arrapahoes were sent after them, but I have not yet heard the result. We are now near the home of the enemy & may look out for them. The Comd is in excellent spirits – every man sanguine of a successful issue. 21 miles today.

48. Bourke identified the informants as three Shoshone Indians who had ridden from Cantonment Reno, where their fellow tribesmen were assembled and awaiting Crook's command. The Shoshones reported seeing trails of the Sioux passing northward toward the sources of Crazy Woman, Clear, and Tongue Rivers (diary, November 17, 1876, Bourke Papers).

November 18, 1876. Powder River, Cantonment Reno

This was McKenzies day to be ahead so I have reveille at 6 oclk. Got out of camp at 7.10 after a very delightful nights rest. I am a good deal troubled each morning by my old cough, the remains of the pneumonia of many years ago, but it is not so bad as many times in N. Y.[49] As soon as I get the mucus from my lungs I am all right & feel excellently well. The road today was down the dry fork of the Powder River, mostly along the bottom sometimes along the very bed. It is fairly good but very crooked. When we stopped to lunch we started a rabbit which took refuge in a hollow log. I twisted him out in North Carolina style with a forked stick – very much to the surprise of the officers with me who had never seen it done before. Arrived at the river soon after 10 am. It is about 1/<3>4 the size of the North Platte at Ft Fetterman, but instead of the clear sparkling stream I expected to find it is a murky, discolored pea soup kind of a stream, almost as filthy as the Missouri itself. The water is slightly alkaline, but better than that we have had lately. Many of McKenzies teams were stuck in the ford, & he came near losing some animals. Profiting by his experience all my wagons got over safely. Camped in bottom near the post Th<is>e Cantonment is garrisoned by 4 Comps of Infantry – comdd by Capt Pollock 9th Infy.[50] The troops are now in tents, but have almost completed a <s>full set of rude log huts, which will keep them comfortably sheltered – though necessarily crowded & rather dirty. The Cantonment is about 3 miles up the River from Old Fort

49. For most of the period between May 1852 and June 1853, then-lieutenant Dodge was on sick leave, convalescing from a severe attack of typhoid pneumonia. He served at posts in the state of New York in 1858–61, 1866–67, and 1871–72 (Dodge personnel file, AGO).

50. The companies attached to Cantonment Reno were Captain Edwin Pollock's Company E, Ninth Infantry; Company B, Fourth Infantry, under Captain Thomas F. Quinn; Company E of the same regiment, under Captain Charles J. Van Herrmann; and Company K, Twenty-third Infantry, under First Lieutenant Greenlief A. Goodale.

Reno.[51] It is a horrible place to be confined at all winter, & I had rather take my chances of an Indian bullet, of freezing or starvation for six weeks, than to have to stay here till spring.

A singular accident happened to my horse just after we got in. The orderly (Cook)[52] had taken the saddle off, & the horse laid down & commenced rolling. All at once he began to groan & appeared in great pain. On examination it was found that he had run a small stick in his eye, splitting the eye ball completely, & entirely destroying it. Distance today 14 miles.

Went to Post at night. Saw Pollock & all the Offs. P. is the most conceited ass that ever existed.[53] He thinks he can give advice to the Almighty, & talks to Genl Crook and everybody else as if he tolerated them. He is only a fair officer, scarcely above the average as a worker & very much below it as a man of sense & discretion. He always disgusts me, & he did it tonight. How he manages to hoodwink such men as Crook &

51. Established as a supply depot on October 12, 1876, by Captain Edwin Pollock, Cantonment Reno was situated on the Middle Fork of the Powder River approximately eighty-five miles northwest of Fort Fetterman. A photograph of the cantonment taken in the fall of 1876 is in Hedren, *Traveler's Guide to the Great Sioux War*, p. 88. As Dodge indicates, the post was three miles south of the abandoned Fort Reno (1865–68).

52. Private Charles E. Cook, Company I, Twenty-third Infantry, had served as Dodge's orderly on the Black Hills Expedition. He joined his present regiment and company at Sidney Barracks on September 15, 1876 (S.O. 187, AGO, September 9, 1876). For Dodge's assessment of his character and his value as a personal servant, see the entry for November 26.

53. Dodge's acquaintance with Captain Pollock reached back to the Black Hills Expedition and likely beyond, to Civil War times; see the journal entry for December 29 and note 185, below. In the summer of 1875 Pollock was assigned by General Crook to establish a new post, known as Camp Collins, in the Black Hills to deter U.S. citizens from trespassing in that region and otherwise to keep the peace. Crook soon learned that he had not selected the right man for the job since, as Dodge put it in his journal for July 29, 1875, Pollock was "weak & vain, & very full of his own importance" (*Black Hills Journals*, p. 153). During his few months of service at Camp Collins, Pollock earned the cordial hatred of the miners in the vicinity, one of whom called him "the most famous wretch that I know of . . . the devil in disguise" (Sidney, Nebraska, *Telegraph*, December 1875, quoted in Brown and Willard, *The Black Hills Trails*, p. 87). For a portrait of Pollock, see Hughes, *Pioneer Years in the Black Hills*, following p. 29.

Site of Cantonment Reno with Pumpkin Buttes dimly visible in the distance (Photograph by the editor)

Sheridan, can only be explained on the principle that he who blows loudest will always find some one to listen –[54]

Staunton asked me to be correspondent for Tribune. Could not see it, but recommended Foote.[55] Had a pleasant visit at Fury's tent. saw Wieting.[56] Goodale stays with me tonight – Shall try to have Devin left here, as he is not fit to go out.[57] The Dr remains at our camp – (Dr Ousley) who is beginning to be a bore. We remain here till further orders

November 19, 1876. Powder River, Cantonment Reno

Up late for camp life. Reveille being at 6. am – went to work immediately after breakfast getting all ready for the next move. About 9.30 Genl Crook invited me to come up & attend a grand pow-wow of the Indians. Went up after a while. Four Tribes – some say six, were represented. The Pawnees Arra-

54. In a telegram of November 20 to General Sheridan, General Crook praised the rapid progress made in rendering Cantonment Reno habitable by troops. Captain Pollock, he reported, was "entitled to much credit for his energetic administration in bringing the Post to this state of affairs in such short time and with the facilities at his disposal" (Powder River Expedition [hereafter cited as PRE] Order Book, pp. 35–36, Bourke Papers). However, Pollock's officiousness and tendency to meddle in matters not properly his own did not go unnoticed (Bourke diary, December 19, 1876; PRE Order Book, p. 37; both in Bourke Papers).

55. Apparently no correspondent was enlisted for either the *Chicago Tribune* or the *New York Tribune*. The coverage of the Powder River Expedition in both newspapers was derivative, in the latter consisting entirely of articles copied from the *New York Herald*. First Lieutenant Morris C. Foote, Ninth Infantry, was adjutant of the infantry battalion under Major Townsend. Foote was well known to Dodge, having commanded a company in the Black Hills Expedition of 1875; see Dodge, *Black Hills Journals*, pp. 185, 200, and passim.

56. Second Lieutenant Orlando L. Wieting, Company K, Twenty-third Infantry.

57. Captain John D. Devin, Ninth Infantry, suffered from bronchitis and severe articular rheumatism and had applied for a sixty-day sick leave (PRE Order Book, p. 27, Bourke Papers). Endorsing this application, Dodge wrote: "Captain Devin is not able physically to go through the hardship of this campaign. He has evinced the utmost pluck and shown the greatest desire to command his company through the expedition. His condition is such however that had he not applied for sick leave I should have felt it my duty to order him to remain behind" (Endorsement and Letter Book, HQIAB).

pahoes, Snakes & Sioux were all that I heard named. These are now all our allies, but the Pawnees & Sioux, <P>Snakes & Sioux have always been at war with each other & the Arrapahoes came in for a share of enmity of all. The[y] were formed in a circle standing The General, myself & some other officers & the interpreters inside. The Genl then made a speech in which he informed them that as they had been enemies he had brought them together. Now they are all soldiers of the United States, going to fight a common enemy, they must be friends & he desired them to make peace with each other – &c, &c. After he got through the chiefs of the tribes came together & formed an inner circle. Three Bears <Ar> Sioux first stepped out & asked the others to begin the talk. "I" said he "will talk last but I will tell you the truth" – "Straight Nose" a very intelligent looking Arrapahoe then came forward & commenced a harrangue.[58]

The Arrapahoe language seems to be spoken by very few other Indians, though they live with the Sioux. Genl C's speech was interpreted to them in the sign language. "Straight
in Sioux
Nose"'s speech was first interpreted ^ to a scout who understood English, by an Arrapahoe who understood Arrapahoe & Sioux. This man then gave it in English to the other interpreters who gave it to the tribes for whom they interpreted Anyone who has ever played the old game of story telling, where each player hears the whispered story from his neighbor on one side, & whispers it to his neighbor on the other side, can imagine what the speech must have been when filtered through

58. Bourke recorded the name of this orator as "Sharp Nose" and described him as "tall, straight, of large frame, with piercing eyes, Roman nose, firm jaws and chin and a face inspiring confidence in his ability and determination. His manners were dignified and commanding, coming nearer to the Fenimore Cooper style of Indian than any I had seen" since his encounter with Apache leader Cochise four years before (*Mackenzie's Last Fight with the Cheyennes*, p. 12). See also Bourke, *On the Border with Crook*, p. 391. A photograph of Straight or Sharp Nose is in Smith, *Sagebrush Soldier*, p. 32.

so many. Genl C's speech was interpreted by four different
& all
men, sentence by sentence, each ^ of whom commenced at the instant he stopped. In such a Babel of language it is only a wonder how any one could understand. The interpreter for the Sioux was a half breed youngster of 25 or more, the son of my old friend Dick Garnett of Virginia, & who went south & was killed in the war of the Rebellion –[59] There were several half breeds among the Sioux rather handsome & intelligent looking men. Among the other tribes there did not appear to be one.

From their faces, I should judge the intellect to run – Sioux,
two
Arrapahoe Pawnee & Snake. The ^ former were all of the same cast of features. The Snakes were remarkable in having every kind of feature – Thick lips & thin lips – straight noses & flat noses – high cheek bones & no cheek bones – every cast of curious agglomeration of feature was presented, but almost all very ugly. The Pawnees were next in general ugliness. The Arrapahoes were very copper colored, more marked in their color than any of the others & not so dark as any except the Sioux, who have some admixture of white blood. I was very busy & could not stay to see the thing out, but I am told the talk ended very satisfactorily, in all shaking hands & vowing friendship.

My old friend Frank White made an excellent speech.[60] This is the man, with whom I was cornered by about 45 Sioux on

59. William Garnett, the interpreter, was the son of a Sioux woman and Richard Brooke Garnett of Virginia, a West Point graduate. The elder Garnett became a brigadier general in the Confederate army and was killed at the Battle of Gettysburg on July 3, 1863.

60. Li-Heris-oo-La-Shar (translated variously as Traveling or Leading Chief) was known to Dodge as Frank White. He had been influential in persuading his people to move south into Indian Territory in 1874 (Grinnell, *Two Great Scouts and Their Pawnee Battalion*, pp. 58–60). Although Frank White was prominent among the Pawnees he was not their "head chief," as

the Loup in 1867. I have given an account of it in my book. He is a gallant fellow & steadfast friend & I am glad to find that he is now Head Chief of the Pawnees. He came to my tent after the affair was over and we had a long talk over old times He tells me that all the Pawnees know me from what he has told them, & are ready to do me any service. I have several times noticed that they look at me very intently and pleasantly as I ride past them on the march, but have always supposed it only the recognition of my being the Big Chief of the "Walk a heaps."[61] Franks story puts a different construction on it, & a more gratifying one ——

Genl C ordered me to move tomorw & I came away from the pow wow early. We have had no end of trouble today with drunken men, & tonight three shots have been fired in camp. I asked Genl C. to shut up the Traders Store, but he being a personal friend (it is said they are partners in a sheep
in Oregon
ranche ∧) of the <suttler> trader refused, & said I could regulate it.[62] So I could so far as my own command is concerned, but I <co>had no right to regulate Cavalry, teamsters & others, not of my Comd, so after standing it as long as I could, I wrote a note to Pollock, Comdg Post, & asked him to

---

Dodge indicates below. Bourke described him as having a "good face, prominent cheek bones, aquiline nose, large mouth, and frank, open eyes, not so piercing as one usually notices among the aborigines. His general expression is that of a far-seeing, judicious lawgiver, one who takes note of all he has seen and whose advice may be relied on. Still, he is no lamb, as the stern lines of his countenance plainly show. If aroused, he would be a bad enemy" (diary, November 21, 1876, Bourke Papers).

61. The Indian term for infantry soldiers.

62. The "authorized trader" who accompanied the expedition was W. B. Adair. Whether he and General Crook were business associates is uncertain. However, Adair's commercial activity did cut into the trade of Tillotson, the sutler at Fort Fetterman, and when in December the latter complained to General Crook, his objections were of no avail (PRE Order Book, pp. 100–101, Bourke Papers).

shut it – which he did – Wrote long letters to Tooty & to Father and Mother. Also a short note to Joe & a letter to Bob Williams.

Just at dark when everything was ready, & I had given my last orders to the Off[icer of the] Day, an order came from Hd Qrs saying that the Command would not leave tomorw. Sent it down, & ordered reveille at 6 oclk again. <Just> About an hour before this order came a courier came in from Fetterman, bringing dispatches for Genl. C. We are all now on the "qui vive" to know if these dispatches had anything to do with the change in the order. McKenzie came to my tent in evening, but remained only a few moments. Had a warm bath at night. It may have been imprudent, but I have not had one since I left Omaha, & I was so dirty that I had to risk it. I feel first rate after it & have written this diary since. It has been a cloudy threatening day & it is now raining, not hard but steadily.

Goodale left us today.[63]

November 20, 1876. Powder River, Cantonment Reno

After I had written up my Diary last night, & was comfortably in bed two red-legged beauties, Campbell & Smith, came in & chinned me for an hour, & drank up nearly a bottle of my whiskey (with a little help from me.) The rain turned to snow & this morning the ground is covered. It is not cold however, & the sun is now, 7.30 am, struggling hard to get out – Evening – Had a good days work. Devin got his sick leave & will go back tomorw – Sent back 20 men, 18 sick & 2 to be discharged.[64]

63. Lieutenant Goodale was ending a short leave of absence. He resumed command of his company at Cantonment Reno on this day.

64. In S.O. 8, dated November 19, Dodge had directed his company commanders to report the names of men who "by reason of sickness, age, or any other reason whatever" might be unable "to stand the hardships of a pack mule campaign." No facilities would be available to carry those who "give out," he continued. "We want in this campaign all the men possible, but no man who is likely to become a burden" (HQIAB).

Has been a very variable day. Principally sunshine – but some rain & near night snow. Went up to Hd Qrs. Bourke says the Genl is waiting for reports from his scouts & Indians. Some have come in with news that the hostiles are going into the mountains. Others are not in yet & we wait for their return. Have not felt very well today – some symptoms of fever – & cold between the shoulders. Am always afraid of inflamation of the lungs. Am all ready to march when the order comes. Indians having a grand old pow, wow near by. No whiskey sold today consequently every thing quiet & orderly. Visited Pollock 9th for a short time. He is an awful & most conceited ass. Pollock 23rd came to see me in evening – also Maj Townsend, & we had a pleasant time together. Staunton returns tomorw to the east, taking our mail. Bought a few more things from Com[missar]y, spent most of the day in my tent, & read Nicholas Nickleby for the 50th time at least –[65]

November 21, 1876. Cantonment Reno

Up at usual time, & went to work. Many papers coming in. Campbell's trouble with Grenough the principal one. Have I think got this all straight. Released Grenough from arrest, had a long talk with him. Induced him to withdraw his offensive letter to Campbell & I hope settled the whole affair satisfactorily –[66]

65. Charles Dickens's novel (1838–39).

66. First Lieutenant George G. Greenough, Fourth Artillery, had been embarrassed and angered by his battalion commander Captain J. B. Campbell when the latter mimicked his limping gait as he marched at the head of his company. Greenough thereupon addressed a letter to Campbell, which the recipient found offensive. The result was a set of charges and specifications against Greenough for insubordination and disrespectful conduct. Greenough retaliated with his own charges and specifications against Campbell, detailing his derisive mimicry and alleging that he was habitually drunk. Dodge, as the commander of both officers, was directed to examine the whole matter and make recommendations. He recommended that "no notice whatever" be taken of Greenough's charges, they being "evidently inspired by malice in the hope of revenge" against his superior. He secured from Campbell an assurance that he had intended no offense against Greenough when he imitated the

Had all my comd on drill today. Did excellently well – skirmish drill alone. Divided the Infy battalions into three for drill & battle. Think I have now got it just right – as the Regiments represented give me 4 battalions of convenient & manageable size. Ordered to march tomorw, & have given directions for an early start. A Cheyenne prisoner brought in today – captured it is said by Sioux.[67] Many rumors as to what he says. That the whole of the Cheyennes will come in & surrender. It would be a glorious thing could we end this campaign with entire success & yet without bloodshed. It is almost too good to hope for. Everyone in fine spirits & hopeful of the best. To bed about 10 – A little snow on ground this a.m. but a fine day –

November 22, 1876. Camp on Crazy Woman's Fork

Reveille at 5. Broke camp at 6.20. Was directed by the Genl to cut across country to the Phil Kearney road.[68] Made it in about 4 1/2 miles of terrible marching. It has snowed three nights in succession, & been clear the same number of days. This a.m. was dark murky & disagreeable with an inch of snow

---

lieutenant's limp, meaning it as merely "a piece of pleasantry." He then convinced Greenough to withdraw the letter that had caused Campbell to prefer charges against him, and there the matter ended (Endorsement and Letter Book, HQIAB; PRE Order Book, pp. 34, 39, 40, Bourke Papers).

67. This young Cheyenne had been duped by Sioux scouts from Crook's command who had pretended to be part of a war party against the Snakes. Once he had divulged information about his band, the scouts captured him and brought him to headquarters. He was from a small party of five lodges located near the head of Crazy Woman's Fork. Contrary to the rumor that Dodge recounts immediately below, the prisoner informed Crook that, once his party became alarmed by his failure to return, they would likely move across country to join Crazy Horse. That Sioux leader, he said, was encamped on the Rosebud River (Bourke diary, November 21, Bourke Papers; *Mackenzie's Last Fight with the Cheyennes*, p. 11).

68. The supply road that had connected Fort Phil Kearney, established in 1866 to guard the Bozeman Trail, with Fort Laramie to the south. Fort Phil Kearney had been located in the foothills of the Big Horn Mountains on Piney Creek, a tributary of the Powder River.

on the ground. The sun rose beautifully with many gorgeous tints, but soon after disappeared, & though the early morning was mild, it became very severe – so much so that the canteens were frozen solid. I got along very well until after 9. oclk when I took my breakfast of a slice of bread & two small bits of bacon (for I cant eat anything when I have to get up so early –) After 9, the wind was extremely trying & I wanted to send back for my cap & furs, but my new Corpl (sent to me by McKenzie) forstalled all by insisting on my wearing his scarf. This made me extremely comfortable. The march was a terrific one. All our previous marches have been greatly over estimated. This one is under estimated – We were told it was 25 miles – & it is 28 if an inch. My Infy were <9>10 1/2 hours on the road & the rear guard did not get in until after dark –

Nice camp – good water fair grass & a sufficiency of wood – Went to see the Genl as to where I was to camp. Was rather taken aback with the information that we cut loose from our wagons here. Recd orders to prepare everything Cut down my Cos to 30 men. Issued circular in regard to details.[69] Indians are supposed to be about 100 miles from us & we <ex>hope to surprise & scoop them in. I dont anticipate it myself – I only hope. Indians killed three buffalo today. No other game. The Cheyenne prisoner caught the day before yesterday is now saying that he lied, as to the whereabouts of <th>Crazy Horse's camp. If he did Crook will hang him. Paid two visits to Hd Qrs tonight Last time 7 pm, Genl C had turned in. Visited Egan and Roach Herald Cor[responden]t.[70]

69. In Circular 3, dated November 22, Dodge informed his command that it would move the next day using pack mules only for transportation of supplies. Company commanders were to select from each of their units the thirty men "most likely to stand the hardships of the campaign" (Order Book, HQIAB). Those not selected would remain in camp at Crazy Woman's Fork.

70. Jerry Roche, the correspondent of the *New York Herald* who had replaced the controversial Reuben B. Davenport. According to Bourke, Roche was "a far more presentable, scholarly, and genial gentleman than his predecessor" (diary, November 21, Bourke Papers).

Invited them to my tent & gave them several. Pack mule business is not pleasant, & we all expect to suffer more or less, but unless the weather gets greatly worse we are all right – We start with 10 days rations Not a long campaign – indeed I fear too short for success – but if we do succeed the greater our credit – There is still a hope that I may spend Jany and Feby in the East –[71] The country is remarkable as to its water shed. Road today most excellent naturally, but made bad by snow. Every body somewhat excited & all eager for a good result. Men very tired with the long march – My horse played out – Send tomorw to Russell for one[72] Met
repeats his
McKenzie who ^ offer<s> to mount me. Expect to get off late tomorw — New deal.

November 23, 1876. Crazy Woman's Fork

High old time today – As soon as it was light I had everybody at work fixing for the pack mules. so urgent was the occasion that rations were issued to men from the general train until after 12 midnight. The packs were generally ready, & the men were commencing to pack in the wagons the things to be left when an order came from HdQrs directing us to pack everything in the wagons & to be ready to move with them as early as possible This was about 8.30 a.m. By a little after 9, I walked over to HdQr to report that I would be ready to move in half an hour. Just before arriving at his tent I was met by an
my
orderly with a note from Bourke informing me that <the> ^ Comd would not move today. I returned at once & ordered the tents to be pitched again, & all made as before. The men were quite delighted & yelled lustily.

71. Dodge was on leave of absence between February 28 and April 30, 1877, passing some of that period in New York City.

72. This was Captain Gerald Russell, who commanded Company K, Third Cavalry.

After we had got comfortably settled Crook came over to my tent & told me all about it. Sitting Bear a Sioux Chief was sent from Camp Robinson to the hostile Camp nearly a month ago. He went to Crazy Horse's camp, which was when he was there exactly where Crook supposed it to be. While visiting there (openly attempting to persuade Crazy Horse to come in) couriers arrived from Sitting Bulls Camp, giving an account of his fight with Miles.[73] It was not much of a fight only one Indian being killed. Sitting Bull had effected a treaty with Miles the former agreeing to come in to a Reservation in the Spring, & nothing being said about giving up ponies & rifles. If Miles made such a treaty he ought to be cashiered for ignorance[74] as that is the common & every year arrangement ^of <with> the Indian Dept. Indians are allways allowed to make peace in the fall, &

73. On October 22, 1876, a U.S. Army force of approximately 400 men under Colonel Nelson A. Miles, Fifth Infantry, engaged some 2,000 Indians under Sitting Bull and other chiefs at Cedar Creek, northeast of the mouth of Tongue River. The army force pursued the retreating Indians until, on October 27, a large number—estimated at between 1,000 and 1,200—surrendered. A smaller body of Indians, still under Sitting Bull, continued northward toward the Missouri River. Miles's own account of the encounter is in his *Personal Recollections and Observations*, pp. 225–28; a fuller narrative is in Greene, *Yellowstone Command*, pp. 92–113.

74. On October 27, 1876, Colonel Miles wrote to the assistant adjutant general, Department of Dakota, summarizing the understanding between him and the Indians who had surrendered. Miles allowed the large body of captives five days in which to obtain meat for themselves and thirty more days in which to proceed toward the Cheyenne Agency and there surrender. With his report he enclosed a copy of the written agreement between himself and the Indians, signed at Camp on Cabin Creek, Yellowstone River, on October 27. This document made no reference to guns and ponies. On October 28 Colonel Miles wrote again, this time to his departmental commander, General Alfred H. Terry, wishing to clarify the agreement: "Bull Eagle [one of the four captive chiefs] was told, and I believe fully understood, that on his arrival [at the agency] he should turn in his arms, particularly the Springfield carbines, and such horses as the Government should require" (Miles Papers). Evidently, as Dodge indicates, some uncertainty persisted about the guns and ponies, though the rumor that the Indians were being permitted to stay away from the agency until spring was unfounded. For a more detailed account see Greene, *Yellowstone Command*, pp. 108, 111.

are thus sure of an unmolested winter, & are sure to go stealing & murdering again in the spring – only to repeat the process from year to year –

Crazy Horse was quite indignant at the news, & said that if all the other chiefs made peace he would do so also, as he had no notion of encountering the whole force of the whites alone.

Sitting Bear left Crazy Horse's camp to follow up the Cheyennes who went into the Big Horn Mountains. He fell in with on Clear Creek, a Cheyenne Indian who was lost from his party & they travelled together. Some days ago he found a fresh trail going toward the Mountains & sent the Cheyenne to find out who made it. The Cheyenne went to the camp of the party, was captured & is now in camp, the Indian captured while we were at Reno –. Sitting Bear waited a day for him, then himself followed the trail which led him to this Comd. He did not know it was here until he got in a days march when
of Inds
he saw a party ^ going like the wind, with information of our presence to the other Indians. Sitting Bear says that about <C>half of Sitting Bulls people had left him in disgust when he talked of peace & were on the road to Crazy Horse who was about moving his camp to Tongue River to meet them. All will then return to the hunting grounds about Rosebud, & little Big Horn. Our trip was thus rendered useless, as the camp we expected to strike will not be there. The main body of Cheyennes are just over the Big Horn Mts, & the Genl thought of gobbling them first if possible. McKenzie with his whole force of Cavalry, & all the scouts & Indians, were ordered to make a dash. They got off today by noon, & are expected to be about five or six days – we waiting here for them. I hope with all my heart they may be successful.

The news taken altogether is I think favorable. We will remain here a week – by that time Crazy Horse & his new Allies will be on Rosebud – settled. They may hear of our approach, & will probably decide to fight us, expecting in the event of defeat to make peace as Sitting Bull has – a peace all in favor of the Indian. I think he will be so assured of our anxiety for peace that he will not run away. Our object is to get a fight, & if we get close to his camp we will make him come in on our own terms, or destroy him. The difficulty is only to make him stand. If he does so he is our meat – If he runs away in time, our campaign will be a hard & unsuccessful one.

My old Pawnee friend Frank White came to bid me goodby.[75] Russell sent me over a horse today – not a very fine one but will answer. We expect when McKenzie returns to march with our wagons to Goose Creek, then strike out with pack mules Had a lazy day. Read Jane Eyre.[76] At night had a pleasant game of whist with Pollock Clark & Anderson[77] – Clark & I together & beat them the odd game in nine. Has been a pleasant day, tho it has occasionally tried both to rain & snow. If good tomorrow will have another drill, & one every good day while here. Three Bear (Sioux) borrowed my field glass to go on scout –

The camp looks like Pittsburg a very fair article of coal having been found, which as wood is scarce comes in good play –

November 24, 1876. Crazy Woman's Fork

<Dod> Up rather late. Nothing to do but wait for McKenzie. He sent back a small party of his Indians whose horses had played out. Genl came over & paid me quite a visit this a.m. Recommended his sending for more supplies, & soon got an order to send a compy as escort to a train to Reno. Detailed Dodge & his Co[78] but before they had made much progress, the order was countermanded.

75. The Pawnee scouts were to accompany the force under Colonel Mackenzie in search of the Cheyenne camp.

76. The novel by Charlotte Brontë, published in 1847.

77. Captain Otis W. Pollock, Twenty-third Infantry; First Lieutenant William L. Clarke, Twenty-third Infantry; and First Lieutenant Harry R. Anderson, Fourth Artillery.

78. In the absence of its regular commander, Captain George M. Randall, Company I, Twenty-third Infantry, was under command of First Lieutenant Frederick L. Dodge. Lieutenant Dodge was not related to Colonel Dodge.

Finished a diary letter to Father & Mother, & also had written a page or two to Tooty, when we learned that no mail would go out. Had Compy skirmish drill of two hours. Took a long nap this afternoon & enjoyed it. Dr. Price[79] and Clark both went out hunting. Dr. got 3 rabbits – Clark 1.

Had a fine game of whist in evening. Beat our enemies five out of nine, as last night.

Genl C. mortally worried about the little attention paid to their horses by my Officers. ["]They deserve to be made to walk.["] The day has been perfectly lovely, & so is the night, tho it is cold.

No news of any kind –

Genl went out after buffalo but failed to find any. One of his Indians got an antelope.

November 25, 1876. Crazy Woman's Fork

Up late – by sunrise – After breakfast I finished a long letter to Tooty, & then feeling the need of exercise took my rifle & started with Dr. Price & Clark on foot, to see if we could find anything. Went about 2 1/2 miles down the river without seeing anything to shoot. Met Genl Crook on horseback & by himself poking in the sage brush after rabbits. He will be picked off some day. He is as reckless as Custer in a different way. Custer was all dash & daring when there was anything to be made by it, in glory, or public opinion. Crook is just as daring, but in pursuits of his own quiet enjoyment in hunting. He will ride out miles by himself or with one orderly, & that, when he knows that hostiles are likely prowling about.[80] One

79. Assistant Surgeon Curtis E. Price.

80. John S. Collins, the post trader at Fort Laramie, commented on General Crook's inclination to hunt by himself, even in regions known to be perilous: "A good angel seemed to hover over this man and he did not hesitate to carry out any plan that suggested itself to him" (*My Experiences in the West*, p. 161; see also pp. 163–64). John E. Finerty noticed Crook's tendency when on the march to precede the rest of his command by a considerable distance (*War-Path and Bivouac*, pp. 55–56). See also Bourke, *On the Border with Crook*, pp. 110–11.

Indian will waylay & shoot at a single man, when five or six will not attack two men.

Soon after leaving Crook an orderly came dashing up looking for him. <*unrecovered*>He came to us very much excited & said that Indians had been seen near camp that the herds were being driven in, &c, &c. We sent him in the direction Genl C had gone, & started leisurely back to camp. Soon after a Sergt. came dashing up & said that a large party of Indians had been seen, & that Egan had gone over the hill after them. Dr. P. proposed we should go to the top of the bluff & see the fun. We started, but were soon passed by a lot of our Indians who dashed up the bluffs, & then became quiet. They evidently saw nothing, so I declined to walk up there for nothing especially as my feet were entirely too warmly clad for the warm day & were hurting me – We came on & about 2 miles from Camp, saw Egan's Company emerge on a walk from the creek bottom. When we were satisfied it was a false alarm. On arrival at Camp we found it so, but it had been lively in camp for a short time. An Infy man killed a buffalo up the creek today. Had drill today. Took a nap before dinner. Called on the Genl after, & after that we had our usual game, with the usual result. We beat them 5 out of 9 – 3 evenings in succession No news from McKenzie

November 26, 1876. Willow Creek Fork, Powder River

Genl Crook came into my tent before I was up this morning – A courier had come in from McKenzie with information that a battle had been fought, yesterday morning. He had taken the village & most of the ponies but the Indians had got into the rocks & bad lands where as Bourke expressed it "One Indian is equal to 10 Cavalry men.["][81] The Genl wanted to take the Inds

81. Early in the battle on November 25 Colonel Mackenzie had directed Bourke to seek out General Crook and request that he dispatch to the scene a force of infantry, "with their long guns, to dislodge the enemy from the rocks" where the Indians were secure from cavalry fire (Bourke diary, November 30, Bourke Papers).

& finish the matter. We talked it over, & finally I was ordered to start as soon as possible with 2 days cooked rations in haversacks – 100 rounds of am –[82] He gave me three wagon mules to each compy for the blankets. We got off at 11.40 am. The snow which fell last night was about 3 inches deep – Fortunately it was a mild day. The men were in good spirits. For 1<5>8 miles they did well, but after that we struck the mountain, & came for 6 or 7 miles over one of the worst trails I ever saw – Up & down long & tremendously steep places – over rocks & through bogs – & all covered with snow. We got in camp at a quarter to 11 – after eleven hours of the hardest marching I ever saw Bivouacked in snow & in the open air Many men straggled, indeed it was simply impossible not to straggle. The trail was so narrow that the Comd had to move in single file. Sometimes it ran diagonally around a steep slope, when if a man slipped, he was out of ranks at once, & had to get in where he could. In going down one almost precipice one fellow slipped fell on his bottom & gliding swiftly forward was set upon[83] by at least thirty men. A whole Co was down in an indiscriminate heap & the swearing was something terrific.

We were blessed with about a ten days old moon – but its light was fitful in the extreme. Clouds were constantly passing over it, & always (it seemed) just when we were in the worst places. The scene was weird & picturesque in the extreme. Far as the eye could reach to the south & east & north only the unbroken snow, wreathed in all uncouth & fantastic shapes by the broken crags & yawning ravines it covered. To the west the huge pile of the Big Horn Mts, here bare & white, there black with its forests of pine. Bad as it all was, everybody (almost) was in good spirits. I felt first rate, & except that I had to walk down all the steep ravines (my horse being smooth shod) & lead

82. That is, 100 rounds of ammunition per man.

83. Dodge must have meant "sat upon."

Site of the Dull Knife battle. Mackenzie's forces charged up this valley. (Photograph by the editor)

my horse at the risk of having him slide on top of me, I got along first rate. I dont like walking at any time, & I took some promenades on that night that I shall remember all my life –

At last we turned the big Mountain which had seemed to block our progress for so many hours, & plunging a thousand feet into a valley came to Willow Creek a large tributary of Powder River. Here we found Genl Crook and his HdQr Guard, & bivouacked.

The Snow was about a foot deep – <possibly> not that on a level, but drifted in the bottom of Creek. We got a little dry willow & made a rousing fire – considering the quantity & quality of the wood. In a little while my orderly – Cook – a private of I Compy had a good cup of coffee which with cold fried bacon & frozen bread constituted our supper, & a most toothsome & enjoyable an one it was. Cook is a character He was my orderly in the Black Hills, being then a private in a Cavalry Compy. He was transferred to the Infy, being ruptured & unable to do hard service on horseback. He has not the slightest idea of politeness – no bump of reverence – never thinks of saying "Sir" to anybody, & speaks of officers as Crook & McKenzie without a thought of giving them their official title.

But he is perfectly invaluable – a splendid hostler, a fair cook an eye like a hawk for game[,] is thoroughly honest – that is he would only steal for me, if I needed anything. He never forgets or loses anything – is always rough & always ready for anything –

Dr. Price & I had arranged to sleep together – & soon had the snow tramped down, & our buffaloes & blankets spread upon it. By a little after 12. midnight we turned in. For a long time I was kept awake by the coffee, but after a while fell into a splendid sleep – about 3 ock am I was waked by the snow falling in my face, but pulling the Buffalo over my head I was soon asleep again –

Distance 25 miles, & near 10 miles further in hardship of travel

November 27, 1876. Middle Fork, Crazy Woman

Up early from our bed of snow & after a breakfast of coffee & cold fried bacon & frozen bread toasted on a stick, we started for the "seat of war" – Followed down Willow Creek for two miles, then crossed. There was no trail & we got along as best we could under the guidance of an Indian, who had left long before us, & whose track (pony) in the snow was all I had to go by. Genl Crook had crossed the Creek a mile above me & struck for the Hills. About a mile after crossing the Creek, I found McKenzies trail We pushed on this rapidly through a very remarkable country of upturned ledges, & grassy vales (like the country about Fort Fred Steele)[84] for about a mile, when I was met by a Sergt from the Hd Qr Guard, with instructions from Genl Crook to countermarch my column. I started my command back, & waited for the Genl. He overtook me soon. He had been met by 5 Indian couriers from McKenzie. The hostiles had decamped the night before, & McK was then returning to camp with his killed & wounded – 1 officer & 4 men killed over 20 wounded.[85] The attack was as complete a

84. Established in 1868 by then-major Dodge, Fort Fred Steele was part of a system of military posts protecting the Union Pacific Rail Road and the Overland Trail. The post was located at a point where the railroad crossed the North Platte River, about fifteen miles west of present-day Rawlins, Wyoming.

85. Estimates of U.S. casualties in the Dull Knife battle varied for a few days; for example, compare the figures in Dodge's own entries of November 29 and December 1. In his official report, dated December 1, 1876, Colonel Mackenzie identified the casualties. Seven men were killed: Lieutenant John A. McKinney, Fourth Cavalry; Corporal John F. Ryan; Privates James Baird (buried in the field), John Sullivan, Alexander Keller, John Menges, and Alexander McFarland (who died in hospital on November 28). Twenty-five men were wounded: First Sergeant Thomas H. Forsyth; Sergeant Daniel Cunningham; Corporals William J. Lynn, William H. Poole, and Jacob Schaufler; Privates G. L. Buck, G. H. Stickney, J. E. Talmadge, August Strick, Isaac McGuire, Charles H. Folsom, James McMahon, Edward Fitzgerald, William Harrison, George Kenney, Henry Holden, Daniel Stevens, Patrick Reardon, Charles Lurig, Charles Thompson, E. W. Ivison, An-Zi (Shoshone scout), Eugene Hall, William B. Smith, and G.W.M. Replogle (PRE Order Book, pp. 51–52, Bourke Papers).

success as could possibly have been made on the ground, but I will defer an account of it until I can get it authentic.

After crossing Willow Creek, instead of going back on our yesterdays trail, I struck straight towards our Camp. Crossed the great backbone between Powder & Crazy Woman by one sharp ascent, a broad Plain of 2 miles, & a sharp descent, & in about 6 miles struck our going out trail on Crazy Woman. Crossed a boggy branch, & went into Camp on a brook that comes into Crazy from the west. Good grass, water & wood plenty.

Bivouaced in the snow again, but had much better & a larger supply of wood. Had a very pleasant evening though we were almost entirely out of provisions. Sent Cook out to beg some Coffee for breakfast. I shall not trust old Smith, (the mess cook)[86] to provide two days rations again – Went to bed about 9 p.m. Men marched well considering – Distance 17 miles.

November 28, 1876. Crazy Woman's Fork

Waked up about 3. am. by the snow striking my face – pulled the buffalo over my head, & slept again. I woke up about 5 to find it clear but terribly cold – one of the very coldest nights we have had.

I had slept enough, & though I was very comfortable & warm enough, I wanted to get up. There was almost two inches of snow on the top of my buffalo & the weight was uncomfortable However, I stood it until reveille. All together I had a much better nights rest than the night before & good enough for anybody. An old fellow like me cannot sleep ten hours like a growing boy – & I ought not to go to bed so early – Got a mighty slim breakfast, consisting of a good cup of coffee, & some frozen bread, toasted – meat all out. Started at 7. am. I did not stop for the Comd, but came directly in arriving here

86. Probably this was Sergeant Thomas Smith, Company G, Twenty-third Infantry.

12. m – My horse slipped into a sitting posture two or three times today, & I was glad to get off of him. Genl Crook got into camp last night. A mail arrived during our absence, & brought me a nice letter from Tooty dated 7th – rather old, but very satisfactory. Also a deed from Jordan to be signed –[87]

Smith had a lunch or dinner ready, & I dont think I ever had a meal taste so <nice>good. Since I have been out, I have had nothing warm except coffee – & a good dish of soup, boiled beef & fried ham, with good biscuit, butter & other condiments was luxury unparalleled – Went over to report to the Genl – afterwards had a little nap. Genl came over just <aft> before retreat & we had a long talk. He thinks the fighting over, & that Crazy Horse will now either surrender, or decamp & hide himself in the bad lands –[88] He is much pleased with his success. McKenzie expected in tomorw with the dead and wounded – Had a good bath at night. Have'nt washed my face while out. Distance 15 miles – Comd got in 2 p.m.

Egan came over to see me at night – & complimented my troops highly. He says that the Infantry did not make all last summer a single march to be compared with that made by my men on 26th – Chambers, who com[man]d[e]d then[89] used to brag of his 40 miles per day, & claimed that his men made 4 miles per hour. I claim only 2 1/2 miles per hour on good roads, but I make as great distances in the same time as he did. He overestimated, thats all.

87. Robert C. Jordan, a prominent citizen of Omaha, was serving as administrator of the will of Dodge's late mother-in-law.

88. The defeated and dispossessed Cheyennes sought out the village of Crazy Horse, who provided them what limited assistance he could. Lacking adequate food and supplies to help them survive the bitter winter, in January 1877 the Cheyennes came in to the agencies, chiefly Red Cloud Agency, and surrendered. Crazy Horse remained at large until May 1877, when, being offered a safe-conduct to Camp Robinson, he and his band also came in.

89. Major Alexander Chambers, Fourth Infantry, had commanded the infantry battalion under General Crook in the Big Horn and Yellowstone Expedition.

I doubt if any men ever made a more difficult march in better time than mine did on 26th. The Genl & all are well pleased with our performance.[90]

November 29, 1876. Crazy Woman's Fork

Slept like a top. The wind got into quite a gale in the night & woke me up for a short time. Several Officers have pronounced against the use of buckskin underclothing on the ground that having once put them on, one could not take them off without a severe cold. I wore my buckskins on the trip, & determined to try them off anyhow – so after my bath last night, I dressed myself as usual & went to bed. Have been about all day & so far feel no sort of inconvenience or symptom of cold. After Breakfast went over to see Genl Crook, as to when we will likely leave here. I want all the Drills I can get.[91] He is going to send the wounded to Reno, & at the same time get an additional supply of rations. <H>We will not likely leave here before Decr 3d. McKenzie got in about 11 am. I went down to see the wounded. They were brought in on Travois, undoubtedly the very best way to carry sick or wounded men, when ambulances are not to be had or where they cannot go –[92] The wounded tell me that this mode of travel is not unpleasant though in rough ground, in narrow bad places there is a great deal of motion. Twenty four poor fellows were thus brought in – one an Indian (Snake) Some of the wounds are severe. One or two may die, & two or three lose legs or arms.

90. Bourke later characterized the rapid movement by Dodge and his troops, "twenty-six miles over the frozen, slippery ground in twelve hours, much of the distance by night," as a "wonderful march" (*On the Border with Crook*, p. 393).

91. Dodge ended this statement with a comma.

92. Bourke in his diary entry for November 30 echoed the views of Dodge concerning travois. In part on the basis of their utility in the Powder River Expedition, the army tested travois for general use in transporting the sick and wounded, but the practice was never widely adopted. See U.S. Congress, House, *Report of the Secretary of War* (1880), p. 322.

All are now in Hospital & have been carefully attended to. They will rest tomorw & next day go to Reno.

We have now pretty authentic information in regard to the fight. The Sioux allies had discovered a village of the hostiles but reported it as 80 lodges, or about 250 fighting men – Genl Crook thought that 700 Cavalry and 350 Indians[93] ought to scoop these in without trouble. McKenzie was therefore sent. He went out 12 miles, & camped – sent out his spies & at night took up his line of march. After passing through a most difficult country for 20 or 25 miles they heard the sounds of the Indian drums. They were having a grand scalp dance He waited until these ceased & then moved forward. The village was situated in a valley bordered on each side by tremendous hills, from which deep ravines cut the valley with deep & narrow canons – (gullies). These delayed the advance very greatly as the snow covered sides were soon slippery as ice.

When McK got within half a mile he was discovered & the war drum of the Cheyennes called the sleepers to arms.[94] Just at daylight he charged into the village – most of the inhabitants of which had already taken to flight – but enough were still left to give the newcomers a warm welcome. He soon got possession of the village which was found to extend for a mile & a half on both sides of a large creek – About one third of the ponies of the Cheyennes were taken by our troops.

By this time the hostiles had got onto the heights & in the rocky sides of the ravines & poured in a heavy & accurate fire on our troops. The short arms of the Cavalry could not compete with the better arms of the savages.

93. Dodge wrote "Indains."

94. According to the *New York Herald*, December 11, 1876, p. 6, this was "a big bass drum . . . which they had as a present from the great father in Washington."

Schuyler (Crook's aid) with the Shoshones[95] had secured a good position on a commanding height & did great execution on the enemy. Charges were ordered & efforts made to oust the Indians from their fortresses, but without success & with loss to us. Lieut McKinney was killed in one of these charges.[96] Then all wished for the Infantry with their long rifles – Finally it was determined to destroy the village. Officers & men were set to work. 173 lodges were burned with all their contents. Buffalo meat, for a winter's supply, robes blankets clothing saddles <r>cooking utensils ropes – everything not carried off by the captors was ruthlessly destroyed. Some arms & ammunition were also found & taken possession of –. The Indians fled from the village in their night gear – Some had not even their mockasins, & some even left their arms – though they generally (the bucks) siezed their arms & rushed out to save their ponies, which is their wealth. They had not any great supply of am[munitio]n & they threw away but few shots – only the best marksmen keeping up the fight. Finally the Indians called out to say that they would surrender if the firing was stopped. McKenzie was either unwilling or unable from the scattered position of his men to stop the firing, & thus a magnificent opportunity was lost. We might just as well had them all prisoners at this moment as not. The hostiles held good their position in the rocks & sides of a great ravine for [*blank*] day. At the end of that time it was found they had decamped

95. In addition to commanding the Shoshone scouts, First Lieutenant Walter S. Schuyler served as one of General Crook's two aides-de-camp.

96. First Lieutenant John A. McKinney, Fourth Cavalry, was ambushed in a charge intended to secure captured horses against efforts by the Cheyennes to recapture them. Acting Assistant Surgeon L. A. La Garde saw McKinney being carried by four men to his medical station. According to Dr. La Garde, the young officer was "shot through the head, one bullet went through his body, one through his arm and abdomen, and one through his spinal column, and yet he could talk." Lieutenant McKinney mumbled a few words to Dr. LaGarde and died soon after (Order of the Indian Wars Collection). A photograph of McKinney appears in Smith, *Sagebrush Soldier*, p. 74; and in Robinson, *Bad Hand*, p. 218.

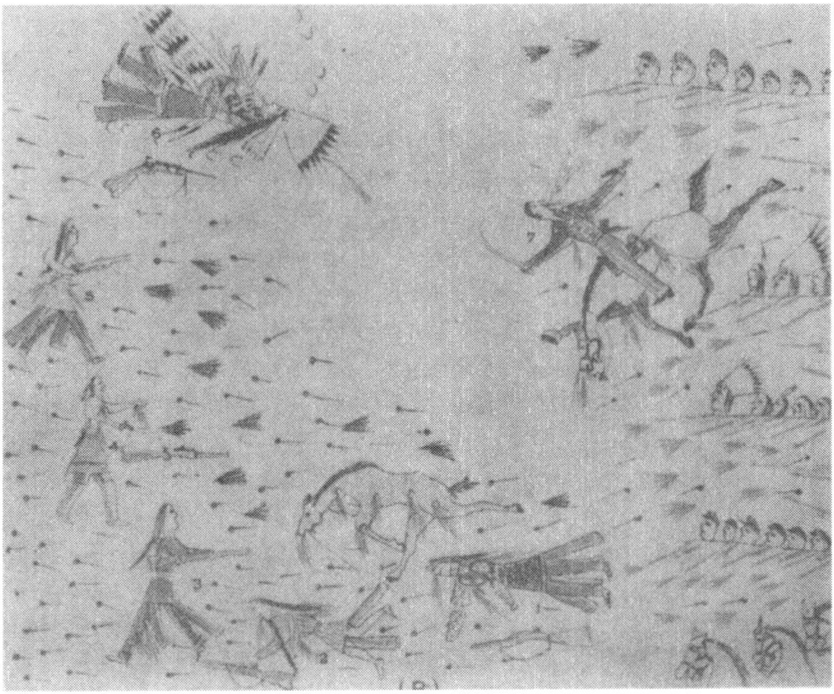

Sketch with colored pencils of the Dull Knife battle by Big Back, a Cheyenne Indian. "Only prominent chiefs who were killed at this fight are represented on the Indian side. . . . The names of the chiefs thus shown are: (1) High Bull; (2) Walking Calf; (3) Whirlwind; (4) White Face Bull; (5) Bull Hump; (6) Old Bull. Short lines with a dot at one end represent flying bullets. The bullet passing through Lieut. McKinney's body (7) indicates the manner of his death." (Dodge, *Our Wild Indians*)

Genl McK thought it prudent not to follow, as the Indians could whip him back whenever he attempted to advance – The Indian loss is irreparable. All their lodges, their winter supply of food, bedding clothing everything except their arms & ponies.

How they can exist in this bitter weather without anything is a problem for them to solve –

Some of their women & children will certainly be frozen. They have still about 1200 ponies in their possession. We got

610 about one third of their herd. These will supply food, & if they can get to other Indians they can barter them for shelter. Six ponies were killed for food the night of their leaving.

Our loss is 1 Officer and 6 men killed & 23 soldiers & 1 Indian wounded. It is the first blow ever struck with effect at this Tribe, the Northern Cheyennes, who have always boasted heretofore that they have never been whipped.

They are the very best soldiers on this continent, indeed I think in the world.[97] It is impossible to fix the Indian loss in Warriors but it is believed about 50 were killed & 100 wounded. There were over 200 lodges – between 1400 & 1800 inhabitants – or about 600 fighting men – for the bucks fight from 12 years old to the grave. It is a tremendous blow to all the hostiles for this tribe has been their head & front. In their village was found ample evidence of their having been in all the fights of the last year – from the Crazy Horse affair of last March – the Rosebud, the Custer & Reno fight – in all.[98] Officers who were in the other fights recognized in this the boom of a huge gun, heard both in the Crazy Horse and Rosebud fights. Among them was a telescopic rifle which did great execution[99] – but a

97. In a brief account of the Dull Knife battle in *Our Wild Indians*, Dodge paid tribute to the Cheyennes not only as soldiers but as a tribe "as brave as ever trod the soil of Greece" (p. 499).

98. Dodge refers, respectively, to the engagement with Indians by troops under Colonel Joseph J. Reynolds, Third Cavalry, along the Powder River on March 17; the battle of June 17 between General Crook and the Sioux on Rosebud Creek, in Montana Territory; and the disastrous encounter of June 25 in which Lieutenant Colonel George A. Custer, Seventh Cavalry, and the companies with him were annihilated by Sioux warriors under Sitting Bull. By "Reno" Dodge means Major Marcus A. Reno, Seventh Cavalry, who with most of his troops survived the Custer fight.

99. In an account by Jerry Roche, Dodge's booming "elephant gun" and the second one so effective at long distance conflate into a single weapon: "One Indian had found a secure place in the hills and played sharpshooter nearly all day with one of Sharp's long range rifles [a preferred gun for buffalo hunting]. The gun must have shot a cartridge containing about 120 grains of powder. Every time he fired the report seemed to rend the very walls of the canyon, echoing like the roar of cannon from hill to hill. Late in the afternoon a cheer went up from some of our boys and the big gun was silent thereafter" (*New York Herald*, December 11, 1876, p. 6).

citizen with our troops had a similar one with which he killed three Indians at almost incredible distances, so we are even on the telescope. The big gun carried a round bullet of about 2 oz – probably an English elephant gun, bought in Canada.

There were also found in the camp five or six fresh white scalps – one a woman's. We do not know when or where they were taken, but it was very recently, as they were on the very night they were attacked having a grand scalp dance in four different locations, in honor doubtless of the killing of the people to whom those scalps belonged – It was probably a party of miners, which had a woman along. The scalps were too fresh to have been brought from the settlements.

Altogether it has been a very successful affair. It might have been much more so had McKenzie possessed as much administrative & political sagacity as he has gallantry in the field. Still it is no time, nor is there any cause for grumbling. The affair stamps our campaign as a success even if nothing more is accomplished — I only regret that my portion of the Comd had no share or lot in the affair. All say that had the Doboys been there not an Indian would have escaped. If I had been allowed to go we would have had a more complete story to tell.

The chances are now that our campaign is virtually closed. Genl Crook starts out the Indians tonight in hopes of intercepting the Cheyennes in their flight towards Crazy Horse's camp. If he succeeds he thinks he can induce them to surrender. Crazy Horse will undoubtedly have pulled foot for the bad lands before we can get to him. He will soon have heard about this affair, & I dont think will stop to discuss questions with us. He may after sending off his women & children stop to give us a little fight by way of bravado, but I do not think he will do so –

Wrote a long letter to Father today. Signed deed & sent it to Jordan. Went to see Genl C. in evening about escort to train. It will not likely go befor the day after tomorw, as the Drs. think the wounded ought to have a days rest.

Started letter to Tooty at night – but failed to finish it – as I propose to make a long one

Thanksgiving Day, November 30. Crazy Woman

Up at usual time. Busy writing letters. Finished a long one to Tooty – also one to Kate Chambless – one to Bob Williams. Went over to Mackenzie's Camp at 11.30 am to attend the funeral of the poor fellows killed in the fight (5) five – One was buried on the field. The affair was most creditable – the whole Cavy Comd attended mounted. All proper ceremonies & honors were paid, & the dead placed in their graves with the solemn words of the Episcopal service – After it was over I, with Townsend & Campbell went to Mackenzies tent. We found him very downcast – bitterly reproaching himself for what he called his failure. He talked more like a Crazy man, than the sane Comdr of a splendid body of Cavalry. He said to an officer that if he had courage enough he would blow his brains out. Townsend & Campbell went out soon, & Mac opened his heart to me. He is excessively sensitive – He said he had often done better with a third of the force at his comd here – that he believed he degenerated as a soldier as he got older – that he was a fool, & ought to have captured every Indian – that he regarded the whole thing as an utter failure. He even stated that he was sensitive lest some one might attribute cowardice to him – & much more of the same kind. He was so worked up that he could hardly talk, & had often to stop & collect himself. I bullied him & encouraged him all I could, told him that he was foolish & absurd to talk so, that we all regarded the affair as a grand success, and that his record was too well known for anyone to attribute cowardice to him I left him feeling much better, but he was in such a state that I thought it right to tell Genl Crook about it. The Genl was greatly worried & soon left my tent, I think to send for Mac & get him to play whist or something. Went over to see Egan and Roach in evening. The Indians were having a war dance & I went down to look at the absurdity.[100] Remained only a little while. Frank White, my Pawnee, came to see me this afternoon. He has been on a scout with 4 others & ran into the Cheyennes – The party got on the narrow rocky top of a high hill – while their enemies passed below – He says they were seen but the Cheyennes were in too great a hurry to make any attack on them.

Frank is a great friend of mine, & as evidence of that friendship, he proposes to bring me tomorrow a part of a scalp. His bucks gave him three scalps. One he is going to cut in two, subdivide one half give me one quarter & North the other – This makes us almost brothers in the Indian idea, & is the greatest compliment he can pay to North & I.[101] North is the Commander of the Pawnees – I dont want the thing at all, but it would be an insult not to accept it. I'll give it to some of the Omaha Indian lovers[102] – Pretty busy today in various ways – reports & returns having to be made. The departure of the train has been delayed until the day after tomorw – the Drs. reporting it best for the wounded – Lieut Dodge & Co I is ordered to escort it to Reno. Dr. Price will go down with them, but return next day. I would not like to lose him – Mackenzie is ordered to hold himself in readiness for a move –

100. Despite his longstanding interest in Native American beliefs and customs, Dodge regarded them as representing a "savage" mode of existence which, as a "civilized" individual, he could not fully identify with.

101. Frank White presented the quarter-scalp to Dodge on December 20; see the journal entry for that date. In *Our Wild Indians*, pp. 513–15, Dodge recounted the ceremony that preceded the presentation of this gift, dwelling on its obvious religious significance to the donor. However, he mistakenly described the incident as occurring on November 30.

102. Despite his sympathy with the plight of Native American tribes whose existence was threatened by American expansion westward, and despite his respect and regard for Indian comrades like Frank White, Dodge evidently did not consider himself an "Indian lover." By this phrase he probably refers to advocates of "sentimental humanitarianism," as he terms it in *The Plains of North America and Their Inhabitants*. Those persons, he writes, are a "large class of most excellent people, [who] conscientiously and most firmly believe, that the Indian is a supernatural Hero, with a thousand latent good qualities, needing but the softening touch of Christianity to develop into a model of all virtue" (*PNA*, pp. 364–66).

what, no one knows but Crook It is too late to attempt to cut off the Cheyennes–

1st Day of Winter, December 1, 1876. Crazy Woman

Slept well & awoke to a lovely day. The weather is superb. Cold at night, but bright & clear & quite warm in the day. Finished up my letters. Went over to Hd Qrs. Talked with the Indians & Hd Qr people. Genl C. was busy getting some Indians off to the Agencies – to induce others to join us.[103] Spent part of the morning studying up my maps. About 3 pm Clark came to me & said that Fury had just informed him that we were to start back to Reno tomorw. I was just going to Hd Qrs to inquire when I met Mackenzie who was coming to my tent. He also had heard something of the move, but had no orders. While we were discussing the probabilities & rather pitching into Crook for his most extraordinary and unnecessary reticence he came in. I asked him to sit, but he said, "I've only a moment to stay. You will march tomorw & should make arrangements tonight for crossing the river."[104] "What river?" I asked. "This" he replied. I said, "I have heard we are to march back to Reno. Is it so?" He said "Yes". Just then Mackenzie made a motion as if to ask a question, when Crook abruptly left the tent without saying "by your leave, or D—n your soul, or any such pleasantry" – as the Irish man had it – Well all calculations are baffled – I went down to Hd Qrs tonight, & enquired around to learn if any scouts are in – None that anyone knows of. It is not then a move founded on recent information. I conjecture that it is merely a change of base.

103. According to Bourke, these seven Sioux warriors were bound to Red Cloud Agency, first, to ascertain whether any Cheyennes had surrendered there and, second, to recruit an additional contingent of auxiliaries (diary, December 1, Bourke Papers).

104. Dodge included an unnecessary quotation mark at the end of the first sentence in General Crook's statement and another at the beginning of the second.

Crook is satisfied that Crazy Horse has left Tongue river & gone into the bad lands about Slim Butte. We will probably strike for the Belle Fourche, with our base on the Black Hills.[105] All right – I dont care particularly where we campaign – one place on these plains is about equal to another, & this new move will place us nearer to mail & friends. The only serious point is that we are also nearer supplies, & this move may materially lengthen our campaign. Orders given & all ready for an early start tomorw – & with this book ends the first chapter of the great Winter Campaign of 1876.[106]

105. Dodge probably meant "in" or "on the edge of" the Black Hills. During the summer of 1875 he had studied the region in order to find a suitable position for a military post. See Dodge, *Black Hills Journals*, pp. 106, 138, 214, 216, 247, 248, 249.

106. Dodge wrote "1867." On the pages that follow he made several entries that are not reproduced here. On p. [67V] is a listing of "Camps & Distances of Marches" between Medicine Bow Station and Crazy Woman's Fork; on p. [68R], written with the notebook in reversed position, is a tabulation of mileages between Fort Fetterman and Tongue River, with points between. On pp. [68V] and [69R] are details of Dodge's mess account from November 5 through January 3, 1877. The last page of the notebook, p. [69V], includes a simple map showing a trail, a mountain pass, and a tributary system of watercourses.

Journal Two: December 2–22, 1876

Powder River
Expedition
Winter
1876
No 2[107]

December 2, 1876. Cantonment Reno

Reveille at 5.30. Broke camp at <6>7.20. Ice hardly strong enough so I built a bridge of logs & poles over it for the men to pass over –

Very cold morning – & the wounded got off late. I remained by my camp fire until 8.30. Came direct while the road was very round about. Killed two Sage Grouse with rifle – wounded another – Ought to have got more. Long and hard march – arrived 4 pm – Comd half an hour later. Camped on the old ground – No mail. Met Frank Grouard[108] in Traders store

107. This manuscript journal consists of eighty-two unnumbered pages in a copy of "Pocket Scratch Book No. 4," a stiff cardboard pad measuring 3 3/8 x 4 7/8 inches, to which are attached sheets of plain unlined paper. Although the pad is designed to permit easy ripping away of its individual slips, in this copy all the original pages are present. On the bottom side of the cardboard pad Dodge wrote in black ink, "Winter Campaign [/] 1876." On p. [1R], "2" is written prominently and encircled in pencil. Except as noted here, the journal text is written in pencil. The text begins on p. [1R]; p. [1V] is blank.

108. Information from Grouard had special value, for he was likely to be apprised of the general's intentions. Finerty reported that Crook "would rather have lost a third of his command, it is said, than be deprived of Frank Grouard" (*War-Path and Bivouac*, p. 64). Grouard was one of the men

while waiting for wagons – Found out where we are going on Belle Fourche, south of Mizpah Creek – on which at last accounts Crazy Horse was encamped. Find only 70,000 pounds forage here – a little over two days supplies[109] – & that alone assures us against any further success. Our animals must break down in a week or ten days without forage. We will however try it any way. It is barely possible we may by this detour catch Crazy Horse napping – & if we do! Very bad news from the States. Rioting & fighting – Politicians will rule or ruin. To bed very early. Saw Pollock for a moment – & went for him on the Coal question. Got a quart of Whiskey as a great favor from Trader's store. Fortunately for the Comd, he is out of that article – Will probably remain here tomorw – Men did well on the march today – & I am well pleased with my Comd. Distance 28 miles –

December 3, 1876.
Buffalo Springs, Dry Fork of Powder River

Genl Crook told me last night that we would probably remain at Reno today – at all events would not start before 11 or 12 Oclk. I therefore ordered reveille at 6.30 & breakfasted at 7.30. I was lying in my bed about 7 waiting for my man to bring water when an orderly came to the tent door to say that the Genl wished me to get my Comd off as early as possible for Buffalo Springs. I was disgusted, but there is no use in being so with Crooks orders. He really does not know ahead what he intends to do. Makes up his mind at the last moment, & then acts at once – expecting everybody else to do the same.

---

dispatched by Mackenzie to Crook's camp to report on the situation and request reinforcements. See De Barthe, *Life and Adventures of Frank Grouard*, pp. 169–70.

109. Estimates of the amount of grain required for the animals with the expedition ranged from 26,000 to 30,000 pounds per day (PRE Order Book, pp. 90, 92; Bourke diary No. 15, passim; both in Bourke Papers).

He has nothing to do but make up his mind. I have to take care of my men. I had clothing to draw & other things to attend to. Had the General[110] at 8.30 & got my men off a little after 9.30. I started about an hour after. It was a very warm day. The ground [? ?]ling with melting snow my horse got tired & I got very tired. On the short march, I was more tired than I was yesterday on the very long one. The Comd got into Camp about 5 pm

Wrote a short letter to Tooty – to send by Courier who left at sun set. Issued a special order regulating affairs on the new departure. I leave a Lieut & 30 men here. It is to be our depot & source of supplies.[111] I send in report of my accounts to Fort Fetterman. Have organized a pioneer party. Tomorw we strike out for ourselves, on an untried route – across to the head of the Belle Fourche & then down that stream. Dont expect we will do anything. Are now short of forage – 10 days 1/2 forage on hand & ground covered with snow. Shoshone Indians left us at Reno. Are going directly back to their country, about Ft Bridger.[112] Have Sioux Arrapahoes & Pawnees with us yet –

110. An assembly call, usually on drums or trumpets.

111. On December 3 General Crook informed the commanding officer at Fort Fetterman that the camp at Buffalo Springs would serve temporarily as a supply depot. In addition to the 200,000 pounds of forage already ordered for delivery at Cantonment Reno, he directed that 200,000 pounds more be sent to Buffalo Springs "with the least practicable delay." On the same day Crook addressed a telegram to Lieutenant Colonel Robert Williams, adjutant general of the department, at Omaha. In addition to the 300,000 pounds of forage that he had ordered sent to Fort Fetterman on November 9, he now required 300,000 more pounds "without delay." Bourke, who drafted the telegram to Williams, wrote: "He [Crook] says for you to take care of your end of the line and see that supplies when needed are pushed through to Fetterman. But from Fetterman on to his own Command he will give the necessary orders as it may be difficult to keep you promptly informed of changes in position of the Expedition" (PRE Order Book, pp. 55–58, Bourke Papers).

112. The Shoshone auxiliaries were anxious to return to their homes, for in the Dull Knife battle they had found evidence that their people had recently been attacked. On their journey home they were accompanied by Tom Cosgrove, the guide and interpreter who had had responsibility for them under General Crook (PRE Order Book, p. 54, Bourke Papers). Fort Bridger was located in the valley of Black's Fork of Green River, in the southwest corner of present-day Wyoming.

Genl killed a new kind of snow bird today – very rich colors. He gave us the telegram of political news. Bad situation. I wish we could be ordered in. If there is to be trouble, I'd like to be on hand. Dr. Ousley leaves us here – Paid me his mess bill – $20. Take Cummings in mess after tomorw.[113] Distance 14 miles – Bad Camp water & grass miserable –

December 4, 1876. Buffalo Springs

Got up late this a.m. with the expectation of getting off about 11.30. Had all my details made & every thing ready for a start. About 10. Oclk went over to see the Genl & was informed that we would not move today. Supposed it due to arrival of train with forage – but when I went over this afternoon to see if we started early tomorw he informed me that we would not move so long as it threatened to storm – That the Indians said a severe storm was coming up, & he did not wish it to catch us on the divide without wood for the men, or shelter for animals. He said moreover that he did not mind the delay as we had plenty of time to do what we have to do – What that is not a soul knows except himself, & I must say it is extremely exasperating to have so very much secrecy about a matter where secrecy can be of no sort of service –

I am sorry to say that I do not believe he has any definite plan or expectation. He proposes to go a certain distance in a certain direction hoping like Mr Macawber that something may turn up,[114] but his actions convince me that he either has no plan, or that it is very illy made. For instance he sent off from Crazy Woman, a lot of Indians to procure more recruits from

113. Acting Assistant Surgeon Owsley was to accompany the sick and wounded men being transferred to the post hospital at Fort Fetterman. Dodge's new messmate, First Lieutenant Albert S. Cummings, Fourth Artillery, was adjutant of the infantry and artillery brigade.

114. Mr. Wilkins Micawber, in Dickens's *David Copperfield* (1849–50), is an incurable optimist, always confident that something will "turn up" to save him from penury.

the Agencies – It will take these Indians at least 8 days to get
10
to the agencies – & not less than ∧ ten days more will be required for those recruits to get to the Little Missouri where they are to meet us – We start from here when this storm is over with rations to the 20th Decr How the recruits are to do us any good, with so small a margin to work on, is a problem for a Brig Genl. I can't solve it – There is nothing of news today. Weiting came on from Reno, & was in camp for an hour or two. He is ordered to take McKinneys body to Cheyenne,[115] & afterwards has 2 months leave of absence. Campbell came to my tent at night and owled me for two hours – taking sundry drinks – Went off at last. "It's a long lane &c &c" –[116]

December 5, 1876. Buffalo Springs

The wind blew terribly in the night & I had some anxiety for my tent but it stood the pressure all right. I slept well, though I was annoyed somewhat at the continued flapping of the fly. After I got up I had it sewed fast to the tent & there is no more flap. We do not move today & the weather was given as reason. It was too thin – Soon after breakfast Crook & Mackenzie came to my tent both in fine humor. An orderly soon after came over with a copy of Sheridan's & Sherman's telegrams congratulating C & M on the affair with the Cheyennes.[117]

115. Accompanied by Second Lieutenant Wieting, the body of First Lieutenant McKinney was to be transported to Cheyenne. From there it was to be sent by express to the late officer's home in Memphis, Tennessee (S.O. 7, December 4, 1876, PRE Order Book, pp. 53, 61, Bourke Papers).

116. "It's a long lane that has no turning"—that is, apparently, even good times must come to an end.

117. General Sheridan's message of December 3, 1876, was simply to transmit with his own congratulations the message of General Sherman on the day before, which read in part: "Please convey to Generals Crook and Mackenzie my congratulations and assure them that we appreciate highly the services of our brave officers and men who are now fighting savages in the most inhospitable regions of our continent. I hope their efforts this winter will result in perfect success and that our troops will hereafter be spared the necessity of these hard winter campaigns" (PRE Order Book, p. 67, Bourke Papers). Bourke also copied these dispatches into his diary for December 4 (Bourke papers).

Mac, was very like himself under the praises of his superiors & was quite jolly. After he went off I boxed Crook on the situation. I told him that I did not ask out of mere curiosity but that if there was no reason for secrecy I wanted to know what were his plans for the next thirty days. To my surprise & pleasure he said there was no secrecy at all, & that he would tell me all I wanted to know. I got the maps & went for him with a lot of questions. We are to march by Pumpkin Buttes to the Belle Fourche & go down that stream to its forks – there strike across to Little Powder River & continue down that to its junction with Big Powder. From there as a center the Indians will radiate in all directions. If they find a village we will go for it on packmules. If not we will return. I carefully estimated the distances with him. "It will take" I said "about ten days for the Comd to reach that point. Allow two days for the Indians to report, & it will be say the 18th of this month before we commence our Pack mule march. Suppose that to last ten days we will get back to our wagons by the 28th. With the utmost expedition we cannot get back to this camp under 6 days – or by 3d Jany. We have rations only to the 31. Dec. Now how can you manage it?" — He said, ["]I want to be back to this Camp by the 28th of this month, & to Ft Fetterman by 31st. If we should strike Indians while on packmule scout anywhere within two or three days march of the mouth of Tongue River, we will go in there & get some rations.[118] If we dont find a village we will come back without the packmule scout.["]

He wishes to be very careful of the men & animals. He has no trouble about rations only about Forage We are staying here not so much on account of the storm but to give the Indians sent to the agency, time to get the recruits & meet us on Powder River – He asked me many questions about the

118. The reference is to the recently established cantonment on the Tongue River, later Fort Keogh.

Famous Indian fighters. Clockwise from the top: George Crook, George A. Custer, Ranald S. Mackenzie, Nelson A. Miles. (Dodge, *Our Wild Indians*)

country between the forks of Belle Fourche & Camp Jenney.[119] It is horrible no wood, grass, or drinkable water & I told him so, but this desert is only 60 miles across. <The>One result of my talk to him, is that Rockwell the Com[missar]y, has been ordered to get 3 to 5 days rations here by the time we get back –[120]

After he left Mackenzie came in, & wanted to know all Crook had told me. I told the story & we went over the maps together. Mac, found that from the forks of Belle Fourche direct by Camp Jenney to Camp Robinson, it is only from 7 to 8 days travel, while from the same point around this way & by Fort Fetterman & Laramie it is 17 or 18 days. He seized the point at once & said that he would urge Crook to let him & all the Comd bound for the Agencies go across that way. He would rather risk the desert of 60 miles, if by doing so he could cut off 10 days march. It is about as near for that portion of the Comd which goes to the R.R. to strike it at Sidney via the Agency, as to return this way. So it is possible even probable, that we will return that way, if on our return to Forks of Belle Fourche we have rations for that trip Those forks are as I said 8 days from Camp Robinson but only 3 from here, & here we get more rations, but no more forage – I ordered Des. lists[121] to be made & left here with the men to be left. Beef cattle were sent for tonight to Reno. They will be up tomorw. We will remain here tomorw, though the storm appears over. A nice game of whist in the evening. I feel a great deal better since Crook unburdened himself.

119. Camp Jenney, the first permanent camp established by the Black Hills Expedition of 1875, was situated on the western edge of the Black Hills approximately 110 miles north from Fort Laramie, where the expedition began; see Dodge, *Black Hills Journals*, pp. 49, 60–61. The Belle Fourche River was about sixty miles north from Camp Jenney.

120. First Lieutenant Charles H. Rockwell, Fifth Cavalry, was chief commissary of subsistence for the Powder River Expedition.

121. "Descriptive lists," itemized listings of military stores and equipment.

The water here – & there is only a small quantity – is very alkaline & really unfit for drinking. Most of us are using melted snow. It is not very good, & is not satisfying, but it is far better than the springs.

There is no wind tonight & it is clear & beautiful. Burke and Schuyler came over to see me this afternoon. Egan is sick.

December 6, 1876.
Gruard Springs,[122] South of East End Pumpkin Buttes

Slept like a top. While dressing an orderly came with "the Genls Compliments & the Comd will move at 12 m." Found on going out that the mules had not been turned out to graze & after breakfast I went over to see the Genl & asked if I might break camp at once as that would give the mules time to graze in the afternoon. He not only consented but hurried off his HdQrs. The General sounded at 8.45, & by a little after 9 I started. The Comd got off about 10. The route followed the divide between two branches of the Dry Fork, & is crooked in the extreme. I have made a map of the March, & country on the last page of this book.[123] The ravines are almost impassable & we were fortunate to get over them without breaking something

By a greater detour to the east we might have avoided all. We are however following a wagon trail. It is called the Montana trail & has been used by Miners coming from Montana to Blk Hills.[124]

122. In a list of camps and distances of march from Crazy Woman's Fork, p. [81V], Dodge corrected "Gruard" to "Grand" Springs, the proper place name. Evidently he had in mind Frank Grouard, General Crook's chief scout.

123. A map on the inside back cover of the journal shows a dotted line that marks a trail, "Fetterman Road." The trail passes northwestward to a point marked "Buffalo Spgs" and thence turns to the east between two river systems until it again turns toward the north. At that turn the trail divides into two, one passing directly northeast, the other east and then north. To the north of "Buffalo Spgs," "Reno" is noted on the map. At the bottom of the page a bit of arithmetic is written with the notebook upside down.

124. This was probably the Sawyers Wagon Road, named after James Sawyer, who had surveyed it in 1865.

At 2.30 pm after a long detour to the South East, we suddenly turned to the North & soon after came to camp in a ravine running a little north of west in which was a spring of water deep & clear, & only slightly alkaline – much better than any we have had for some time past. Better even than Powder or Crazy Woman. There is also very good & abundant grass, but no wood. Below us the Indians got some wood, & but that we brought plenty with us, I guess we would have found some. I got into a most comfortable & sheltered nook. The day has been lovely, & the march an interesting one, over the Crookedest road in America.[125] Only a few crossings but they were bad. Pioneers did well. Distance about 11 miles. Pumpkin Buttes near us, North.

December 7, 1876. Belle Fourche Springs

Reveille at 5.30. Slept badly – due somewhat to coffee, somewhat to loose mules – Smith & Cook amused themselves by quarrelling – D—ing each other in the middle of the night. Kistler my special man made my fire about 4.30 am & called me to breakfast by 5. I abused him & tried to sleep, but soon the bugles sounded & I got up. Had breakfast & mounted my horse by daylight – in fact it was too dark to see the track of the pioneer wagon – so I had to go & hunt the road. Had not gone a quarter of a mile before I found a Pawnee wagon overturned – a precursor of what was in store for us – Got started at 10 minutes to 7. am. Went directly north, & after a little over a mile came to Clark & the pioneer wagon turned around & at a halt – The guide, who had left the road, saying that he knew a much better route, had confessed himself lost, & had started out to assure himself of his position. I forgot to say that when I got up it was snowing fast, & at this time, a dense cloud overhung everything so we could hardly see

125. The capitalized "Crookedest" is surely a pun on the name of General Crook.

Pumpkin Butte. Genl Crook came up just then & wanted to know what was the matter. Clark explained. The Genl was non-plussed. The route before us looked fair, but there was no telling what was ahead, the road was to our left rear. I put in my oar, by saying that twas no weather for trying experiments. So he gave the order for the wagons to turn back & take the road – We were then at the east end of Pumpkin Butte. The road ran west to the west of the Butte then turned north. The genl with his Hd Qr G[uar]d struck across country to go around the Butte to the South. I felt equal to the task of piloting my Comd & struck to the north of the Butte, across country – Just in front of where the wagons turned back was a nasty arroyo, which we crossed and started on a course. When we had gone about a mile, Frank Grouard the guide, (not the one who got lost) overtook me. He said that it was all plain sailing in front, & went ahead. In a short time I saw a man on my right, who I thought was he. I sent my orderly after him, & presently he bec[k]oned – I went to him and found him on the brink of a nasty chasm 50 to 60 feet deep, & so steep that a man could not cross. By going to the east he found an old trail & we managed to get over one branch of the chasm, & were then obliged to go along a narrow back bone between the two, sometimes scarcely three feet wide, & with great pieces ready to tumble off on each side into the abyss – I rode over this trail, but I confess to certain nervous tremors. The other off[icer]s walked over & led their horses. Men got over all right. After passing this place we had no trouble – though in coming down into the arroyos of the Belle Fourche, we had to cross two or three nasty places. While crossing the last one I heard many shots & yells, & while going up the bank a Citizen dashed past me, his horse at a run – When I got on top, I saw a Black Tailed deer, running across my front about 150 yards off. I was terribly bundled up, but I jumped off my horse & got out a couple of cartridges. By this time the deer had seen the Citizen ahead, & dashing into the ravine, ran almost directly towards me. I waited until he was about 60 yds off & fired. He fell, but jumped up again. Again I fired & he laid down in the ravine. I went up & cut his throat. My first shot had broken one hind leg, & gone through the other – almost spoiling both hams. However he has lots of good meat on him besides legs.

In a few hundred yards after this we struck the road. Genl C. had passed but the train was nowhere to be seen. From this point the road runs nearly north, & is very good – except an occasional bad ravine. We got to camp at 3 pm, & waited until near dark before a single wagon got up. Then came Genl C's HdQr wagons, & soon after mine. It is now after 9. p.m. & some of the Company wagons are not in yet. Gave Wheaton & Pollock a supper,[126] as their wagons are not in. After my supper about 8. pm I went over to Genl C. to remonstrate with him on the bad management of the trains. He had gone to bed. So I pitched into Fury, the Qr. Mr. He made so many promises of improvement that I could not scold much. The fact is the mules are played out. They are kept in harness from daylight till dark – then tied to a wagon pole until daylight again. Not one has been curried or any other care taken of him since we started, & they are expected to do all the work on half forage of grain –

We expect tomorw to strike wood water & grass, & from what Rockwell the Com[missar]y, tells me today there is another change in General C's programme. We are to lay over after tomorw for four days, to send back for more sub[sisten]ce stores –[127] However good a soldier Crook may be, he has no

126. Captains Charles Wheaton, Company G, and Otis W. Pollock, Company C, both of the Twenty-third Infantry.

127. On December 5 First Lieutenant Rockwell had written to the commanding officer at Fort Fetterman, calling for ten days' worth of complete rations to be sent without delay to the camp on Dry Fork, Powder River (i.e., Buffalo Springs). Four days later General Crook directed the post commander and also the officer in charge of the supply train to forward rations and forage to the camp then occupied by the command, on the Belle Fourche River (PRE Order Book, pp. 69, 73, Bourke Papers).

administrative ability whatever. He well knows that this part of the expedition must be a failure, if for no other reason, because we cannot transport our supplies. His train is in wretched condition yet he does nothing to <keep> get or keep it in order. He might be a cavalryman, for his carelessness of his means of transportation – Mules are the very first element of success in such an expedn as this – yet he seems to care nothing whatever for his mules – The Cavy horses & Indian ponies are giving out every day, & by the time we reach the mouth of Little Powder, it will be a miracle if more than half of us, do not have to walk back. Yet he pushes on – I would not say it out loud – but I think he is pushing on now simply from vanity. It will look well, to go on – no matter at what cost of life or property. He will come to great grief some day, from this trait of character.

There seems to be plenty of small game here, rabbits & sage grouse – but I had no time to hunt & no shotgun. The pioneers killed 2 antelope and an Officer 1 today. The Indians also killed some game. Had a good supper. Wrote my journal. Smith, Off[icer of the] Day,[128] sent in for permission to come in. Is 3 1/2 miles out, & several teams are broken down. Sent him word to come in. I must take care of my men – even if we lose some stock –

Distance today 20 miles – Good water – standing in holes – no wood – grass very poor – plenty of sage brush – for both fuel & forage – Terribly bad day – snow sleet & wind – all day —

December 8, 1876. Belle Fourche

Reveille at 6.30, to give to my belated travellers a chance to rest – started 8 am. Very cold – with a little snow. Road

128. Captain Frank G. Smith, Company H, Fourth Artillery. As officer of the day, Captain Smith had charge of the camp guard.

for ten miles very good then crossed a lot of broken country with bad ravines –

A great deal of game killed today principally antelope & by the Indians, though Officers & men got five or six. I was in rear taking it easy & got no shot, except at a Jack Rabbit which I killed. Our mules are nearly played out, having to work from daylight until after dark, & then are tied up to the tongue of a wagon – When I got to the camping place, Crook wanted me to go a mile & a half beyond. I told him that my wagons could not make it before dark He was rather cross & said that my teams were broken down hauling wood, & that Fury had ordered a lot of wood thrown off. I told him I had ordered no wood to be carried, & that my Qr. Mr. had not reported any violation of the order – &c. &c. After I had selected & got my men into Camp, I went over to see him, & talked quite freely on the mule question – told him their condition, of their lack of food, of their constant work & no care – that by his order I had nothing to do with them & could not give an order to a teamster. He said he knew the condition of the animals, that he had a certain problem to work out & had to do the best he could with his materials. I could'nt tell him so, of course, but he does not do the best with his materials – He takes no sort of care of his transportation. Fury has impressed him with the idea that he is a wonderfully good Qr. Mr. while the fact is he is as poor an one as I ever saw.[129] He is no doubt a good indoor Qr. Mr. but he leaves the whole management of his train to understrappers, who neglect it entirely. No mule is ever curried – some of them are cruelly beaten – they get no grazing, because he is too tender with his teamsters to make them go on

129. In *Mackenzie's Last Fight with the Cheyennes*, Bourke expressed admiration for Captain Furey, with whom he had served in Arizona, as "our efficient and amiable, that is usually amiable, quartermaster." According to Bourke, in the course of the campaign Captain Furey endured much criticism for conditions he was unable to control, being "hauled over the coals by the general commanding, growled at by the battalion commanders, sneered at by the captains and damned by the lieutenants" (p. 7).

herd – Altogether the transportation of this expedition, is the very worst managed I have ever seen, & if for no other reason the expn must be a failure.

I find there is no sort of use in talking to Crook & it really seems sometimes as if he expected a failure, & intended to lay the blame on the failure of his means of transpn.[130] We might just as well go in now, but his pride will make him kill a few hundred animals first.

Wagons get into camp just at dark. Poor camp. Very little wood, no grass, & water alkaline & bad – Distance 18 miles – road rough —

Had a long talk with Crook & Frank Gruard as to the best route to the Rail Road. Frank says he can take us to Fort Laramie by a good route in 8 days. I am pretty sure we will return by Black Hills. There is some talk of sending back for more rations – but Crook said nothing about it – We have now only about 10 days, & must send back or go in to Fort Laramie very soon – Camped in 4 in. snow.

December 9, 1876. Belle Fourche

Reveille at 6:30 – started 8. am. This march is only to find a good camp. Marched down the Belle Fourche. 1 1/2 miles below our camp of last night came to the large fork from the

130. In an interview on December 9 General Crook asserted that he did not consider his winter expedition a failure. "I do not anticipate obtaining any great success for the balance of this campaign, measured by tangible results," he told a correspondent. "But I do expect to so annoy and worry the hostiles as to make it evident to them that they are having the hot end of the poker. . . . The country I am going to is the winter quarters of the hostiles, and has hitherto been exempt from attack during that season. When they see that it makes no difference to us, and that we will be after them in all seasons, they will begin to appreciate their status. The campaign will be necessarily short. Our animals cannot get along without forage, and the supply is limited, with no means of replacing it. We are too far from a railroad" (clipping in Bourke diary No. 17, marked as from Cheyenne *Sun*, December 28, 1876, Bourke Papers; the same text appeared in *ANJ*, December 30, 1876, p. 325, where it was attributed to "the *Tribune* reporter").

South East. Marked on the maps. The route was as bad as could be –

The hills on each side are a curious combination of red sand stone & bad land formation & there is no getting over them. The wagons had to keep the bottom where there is any, & struggle over the spurs of the hills as best they could. The difficulty was that we had to cross the Belle Fourche many times. It is a nasty gulch, with banks from 20 to 30 feet high. Getting down and up these banks was work indeed. We came only 5 miles, yet some of the wagons did not get in until after dark. My Command got to Camp before 11 Oclk but all my wagons were not in until near 3 pm – My own were among the last – Had half a row with Fury about the management of affairs but have finally concluded that I can do no sort of good by quarrelling – I am not responsible, & there is no sense in making enemies. I can stand it as long as they can – so "let her rip" — I shall say nothing more.

Soon after my arrival orders for details came pouring in, so I knew that something was up. Went over to Hd Qrs at night. Saw Bourke & got orders to send one compy to escort a train back to our Depot at Buffalo Springs to bring up all the supplies & troops left there. I detailed Capt Jordan of 9th with his compy –[131]

From what I can hear it seems likely that we will strike across to the Black Hills from here. Indeed it is almost sure that such is now the intention – Bourke told me that if the train sent in did not find at Buffalo Springs the train sent to Fetterman for supplies, a courier & an Indian would go on towards Fetterman, meet the train & take it across country

131. On December 9 Dodge ordered Captain William H. Jordan with his Company A, Ninth Infantry, to accompany the wagon train to the supply camp at Buffalo Springs (S.O. 19, HQIAB). Captain Jordan was to load all stores at the temporary camp and break it up, returning to the main command with the officers and enlisted men who had been on duty there (S.O. 8, December 9, 1876, PRE Order Book, Bourke Papers).

towards Inyan Kara[132] Distance today 5 miles – Good camp – plenty of wood & water, but grass is very scarce –

December 10, 1876. Belle Fourche

Up late – at about 7 a.m. as we do not move today – Went over to see the Genl, but he had gone out somewhere. Passed a very quiet day. In afternoon had my Hd Qr tents moved up on the plateau, as the bottom which I first selected, is, from the warm weather & melted snow, a mass of sticky mud. It got very hum drum in evening, so I got out one of Fred's old novels – Shirley – [133] & read until late. I dont think much of it. A good many brilliant thoughts, but the people are all unnatural. I have often tried to read it before, but as often failed.

All quiet. Jordan left early this morning, before I was up. Didn't see him. Sent all our stock out grazing. Lovely day – warm & balmy though the morning was cool. Nothing new.

December 11, 1876. Belle Fourche

Was waked up about 2 am by the Off.[icer of the] Day, who informed me that a party of miners returning from the Black Hills to Montana, & which passed us yesterday about 1 pm going towards Reno, had been attacked by Indians at our Camp of 9th – their stock and everything taken from them –
had just come in
<&> ^ asking assistance – I refused to believe the report but was answered by one of the men – (two had come in –) assuring me that he was telling the truth. He was in his stocking feet, and had no coat – & the other tho' he had shoes

132. Bourke's information to Dodge summarizes the two orders he had dispatched on this day, from General Crook to the commanding officer at Fort Fetterman and to the officer who commanded the escort to the supply train (PRE Order Book, p. 73, Bourke Papers).

133. The novel by Charlotte Brontë (1849). Fred is Dodge's son, Frederick Paulding Dodge (1859–1937).

had neither coat or pants, & both were shivering with cold & fright. They had come in this plight five miles. I bade the Off[icer of the] Day take them to Genl Crook – & still incredulous went to sleep again. The Genl sent out early this morning & found the story only too true. There were eleven men – they were travelling with two light wagons – one <with> drawn by 4 horses, the other by 4 oxen. They camped 5 miles above us – turned out their stock, made a big fire, cooked their supper & all turned in, not a single man being left as guard or sentinel. About 1 a.m. 5 Indians (as appears from the trail) stole noiselessly into their camp, & opened fire on the sleeping forms. All sprung to their feet & made off into the darkness except one. By daylight all had got into this camp, except that one. The party sent out to assist, found the body of that one stark & cold. He had had his leg broken by a shot, & the Indians had then seized an axe, & split his head open. He was still lying where he had gone to bed – not having been able to move after the shot. The Indians had taken the horses & cattle – all the ammunition they could find & a few articles of little value. They knew evidently that we were near, for they wasted no time but started south at once. Our Indians after a careful examination of everything around, came in and reported. A party was sent out to bury the dead man & a party of Arrapahoes sent on the trail. They can never catch the rascals I doubt – There are several opinions as to what Indians did this, for so small a party, very daring deed. My opinion was that it is a party of Agency Indians who have been following these miners from the Black Hills. For this same party of miners was attacked thirty miles North East of here four days ago, & six ponies taken from them – As the hostiles were on foot & seemed to come from the south, the friendly Indians are of the opinion that the daring rascals are Cheyennes, of the very band we so injured on 25th ult., & who are now following us in the hope of revenge on small parties, stragglers &c – This view is somewhat confirmed by the fact that one of the hostiles lost his mockasin in the confusion of the fight & not being able to find it in the dark left it. It was nothing but a piece of raw buffalo hide, which had been put over the foot, & tied around at the ancle. I have very little confidence in such signs as indicating Tribes, as all Indians after committing a depredation or outrage, leave, if they can, some distinctive article belonging to another tribe, so as to shift if possible the suspicion from themselves. But in this case it seems possible the Cheyennes are the rascals. Their being on foot, is one evidence that way, their coming from the south on our trail another – & the mockasin another, since buffalo are very scarce out of the mountains at present, & their being none toward the Agencies –[134]

The fate of this man, & the party, illustrates a peculiar phase of character of the large majority of the men who risk their lives on the frontier mining, trapping or prospecting. They are brave to imbecility or stupid beyond expression. A few men, possibly comparative strangers to each other, band together & agree to go to this or that place. Without apparently the slightest concern, they plunge into unknown wildernesses, & through countries swarming with treacherous & deadly Indians. They travel without order & without care. If while hunting one should discover Indians, he rushes back to his party, which flies if it can, or fights with courage & tenacity if necessary. Arrived at a camping place they turn out their stock, get supper & go

134. In his diary for December 11 (Bourke Papers) Bourke wrote a detailed account of this incident that agrees at most points with Dodge's. According to him, two miners, not one, had knocked at General Crook's tent asking assistance. At first their story had "an air of improbability," he noted, for "near the place spoken of [as the site of the night attack] is a thick vein of coal our blacksmiths have been using . . . and until about the very hour mentioned, Major Furey had wagons busily employed last night conveying loads of coal to camp." But the Pawnee scouts confirmed the miners' account. Bourke considered that the five perpetrators were "undoubtedly part of the village, destroyed by Mackenzie and had taken up our trail in the hope of finding just the kind of good luck that befell them." Six of the destitute miners—Michael Nolan, M. A. Malone, James Lewis, D. Hunsdon, J. C. Smith, and Fredrick Ferdinand—were issued blankets and rations and permitted to remain with the expedition (PRE Order Book, pp. 78, 79, Bourke Papers).

to bed as unconcerned as if no dangers were around them. If jumped they have no chance & lose all, & as in this case, were we not here by the merest chance for them, not one would likely escape alive –

I once when travelling with a train & troops, came, on the high wide prairie, suddenly on <a>the form of a man, lying on his stomach & sleeping profoundly. He was at least 30 miles from any road & in a very dangerous country. I called to him loudly. He sat up & gazed stupidly for a moment or two, then smiled & seemd relieved. "Where do you belong?" I asked. "I come from Iowa["] – he answered. "What are you doing here?" I demanded very peremptorily. ["]Oh I am looking for work" he said genially. I thought at first that he was a lunatic, but further questioning satisfied me that he was only an ordinary plains lunatic, that is, one who feared no danger, because he saw none. This man had no arms, no bedding, & not a thing to eat – yet was unconcernedly going to certain death had I not found him gave him to eat & told him where to go.

Another wonderful peculiarity of these adventurers, is that they plunge into any wilderness, undertake any journey, without map or compass & without the slightest knowledge of the Geography of the country over which they are to travel. It would seem that Providence has special charge of these people as of children, idiots & drunkards – but this is only partially so – Many parties get through all right as by a miracle. These we hear of & wonder at. We never hear of the great number of parties that dont get through & which disappear & leave no sign. The great majority of these men are outcasts & vagabonds long bereft – self bereft – of all ties of blood or kindred. They disappear from one section. If they turn up in another all right. If not, there are no anxious friends to wonder why, or to institute inquiries – They disappear & that is the last of them. The how, the why & the wherefore are never known, because never inquired into – The poor victim of last night, was buried where he lay, & I doubt if any one in this camp even knows his name.

About 12 m, an orderly came over from Hd Qrs & handed me a letter mail for my Command. One living all his life surrounded with the comforts & conveniences of civilization cannot realize the feeling with which a wanderer in the wilderness looks over a package of letters. To me this mail was indeed a blessing. Two nice letters from Father & Mother, assuring me that all my loved ones south are well. Two from Kate Chambless loving & kind & grateful. It is a true pleasure to have it [in] ones power to do good to such a woman as Kate. She fights her hard battle of life so nobly & so well. She is so truly a true woman – so economical – so proud so managing – so self reliant so independent – so grateful & so loving, that I wish constantly I could do for her a great deal more than I can ever hope to do.

She had received the $300 I sent her to buy a part of her Father's homestead but the sale was put off until next year. She has lent the money to Mr Parker at 8 per ct – a very good disposition of it as the interest will help her.

Two letters from Blackmore noble friend – who flatters me on my book – & tells me it is out Novr 2d & that I will be proud of it.[135] One long letter from Fred, written in very good style but abominable hand. He is well studying hard & is in good spirits – & last & best one from Tooty, loving & kind full of fears for my safety & hopes of my distinction – inconsistent but womanly. A most satisfactory & delightful mail. There is no news, & as yet no President. I hope & trust all this political warfare may end without bloodshed & that when we return we will find all settled & peaceful. It is bad enough to fight

135. The publication of Dodge's book in England had been postponed several times owing to the dilatoriness and ill health of its editor, the English lawyer and land speculator William Blackmore (1827–78). Blackmore's estimate of the publication date was overoptimistic; the book was offered for sale in London on November 23, 1876.

Indians. I hope brothers hands will not again imbrue themselves with brothers blood.

An order came this pm for one of my Battalions to march tomorw. We go down the creek a few miles hunting a better camp I take the Artillery Battalion that having but 4 Companies. The water is bad here & the snow which we have been melting for drinking purposes is fast disappearing The day has been warm balmy & beautiful. Such Winter Campaigns as this we can stand. But I fear me we will pay for it soundly.

December 12, 1876. Belle Fourche

Reveille at 6.30 – Got off at 8 – with General Hd Qrs & the Arty Batn. The Infy were left behind, there being not enough wagons. Stopped for half an hour with Mackenzie, & had a pleasant visit. Marched only about 5 miles went into camp. The creek is a running stream and full of beaver – a large dam & house is directly in front of us. Road generally good but there are many bad ravines to cross. Our wagons unloaded & returned at once to bring up the Infy, which will be here tomorw a.m. Disagreeable nasty night – snow sleet & wind. Played whist with Campbell against Smith & Clark. Got beaten the long rub. Campbell dont know the game. Distance 5 miles.

December 13, 1876. Belle Fourche

Got up at usual time & had a good breakfast. Some of my staff were very anxious to route out some beavers which have built a large dam & house just opposite where we are encamped & came to me for assistance in the performance. Went with them and gave advice. The dam was first cut so as to let the water off sufficiently to enable us to find the entrance to the house. After an hour or two this was accomplished. The entrance was found & stopped up, & they went to breaking into the house, a most tedious labor. However after an hour of hard work, they got an opening, & found *no* beaver. The cute little rascals had evacuated the premises yesterday, the noise around & above them showing them that they were in danger. They had a good sized house & the bedroom was sufficiently large for a man to lie in comfortably. It was about 4 by 6 feet with a ceiling about 3 feet high. I also tried to fish through the ice, but either there are no fish or they were frightened by the noise around them & the rush and rapid fall of the water – Got no bite –

Some time after I got back to my tent, Genl Crook came in. He was in a most amiable humor, & talked very freely & pleasantly. He expects the Sioux scouts every day now, & also some spies whom he sent into the hostile camp. He will not take any risks of roaming about scouting the country with this command. If he can find the hostile camp, & it is within reach he will strike it. If he can not find it, or if it is too far away, he will go in.[136] I think he takes a very sensible view of all the facts, & I expect I have done him injustice in thought. He did not leave until I was called to dinner at 3 1/2 p.m. Today has been very pleasant, clear but cold – & it has clouded up again tonight & the wind blows sharply. Townsend & the Infy got in today & are camped just above us. Mackenzie moved down the river a few miles for grass. Whist at night & got beaten soundly – wretched hands –

Thursday, December 14, 1876. Belle Fourche

Got up & had breakfast at usual time – very cold last night with some snow. Woke up with the cold, had also a little touch of breastpang & Earache – but soon got over all of them. Am Presdt of a Gen[era]l Court Martial convened to try a young officer of Mackenzies Comd named Otis – The offence amounts to but little & Mack had much better have given the boy a good

136. This was the essence of General Crook's plans as he had summarized them to Dodge on December 5; see the journal entry for that date.

sco<u>lding or a weeks arrest.[137] It is absurd to try Officers for every little offence. It only hardens them, & renders them careless of any shame of being before a court – The Judge Advocate (Lee 9th)[138] is slow, & the accused slower. We met at 11 am worked to 3 pm. – finished presentation, & adjourned to 6 pm. Met & worked to 9 pm, & have nearly all day tomorw to work at the same case. Three other cases – soldiers referred to us.[139] Am in a d—l of a snarl for I do hate a Ct Martial of all things The day has been delightful cool clear & bracing. No news – Indian scouts not yet heard from – I mean those from Agency – The spies not yet in. Not a pound of grain on hand, & less than a weeks rations. We are looking anxiously for the train. It ought to be here on 16th I think our expedition draws to a close – without any good result to me –

December 15, 1876. Belle Fourche

Out of bed, & breakfast late. At half past ten went over to Hd Qrs for Court Martial Found everybody excited over arrival of Suttler with 5 barrels of whiskey – which though a good thing

137. Second Lieutenant Harrison G. Otis, Fourth Cavalry, was charged, first, with neglect of duty and, second, with disrespect to his commanding officer. The alleged offenses had occurred on December 10 while he was in command of Company M, Fourth Cavalry, in the absence of its regular commanding officer, First Lieutenant Henry W. Lawton. Otis was rebuked by Colonel Mackenzie for neglecting to see that his company's horses were watered at the proper place. Otis replied to his regimental commander: "I am not in command of the company, but Lieutenant Lawton, and I get all the fault found with me." According to Mackenzie, who filed the charges, Otis's words were not only disrespectful but "without any foundation whatever in fact" (G.O. 3, December 18, 1876, PRE Order Book, Bourke Papers). Bourke's view of the whole matter agreed with that of Dodge. The alleged offenses, he thought, were "of no great import, some little infringement of discipline and nothing more" (diary, December 14, 1876, Bourke Papers).

138. First Lieutenant Jesse M. Lee, Ninth Infantry.

139. These were Private Frank B. Howe, Company B; Private Richard Ghalerger, Company D; and Private Joseph Fountain, Company D, all of the Fourth Cavalry. The men had been charged with violation of the Seventeenth Article of War, forbidding wilful damage to or destruction of government property issued to them.

is likely to do us damage. Court met about 11 am The accused slower than a turtle. Had to bully him finally – or we would never have gotten through Closed his defense about 12 m, & the Court adjourned 'til tomorw 11 am By this time the Suttler had his tent pitched. I went over to see him, & and soon after issued orders prohibiting the sale of liquor by drink or quantity to any enlisted man – but authorizing Compy Comdrs to buy whatever their men needed –[140] I shall try hard to keep my men sober, but am doubtful if I succeed –

Came back to my tent & soon after General Crook came over to pay me a visit. He was very affable & chatted quite freely, though I could see that his object in coming was that I should not be too stringent on the sut<t>ler. However he gave me considerable information. Randal has arrived at Reno with 76 Crows, but has to wait there a few days to recuperate.[141] The 23d Infy is ordered to Dept of Missouri[142] & I am more than

140. In Circular 4, issued on this day from Dodge's headquarters, the officer of the day was instructed to post a guard of at least seven men at the sutler's tent to maintain order. Disorderly and intoxicated soldiers were to be arrested and taken to their company commanders. Upon the closing of the sutler's tent at retreat, a guard was to be maintained outside it, and enlisted men found nearby were to be arrested (Order Book, HQIAB).

141. Captain George M. (Jake) Randall, Twenty-third Infantry, had reached Cantonment Reno after a thirty-one-day march from the Crow Agency on the Musselshell River in the Judith Basin, Montana Territory. He had left that place accompanied by 200 native auxiliaries, but winter storms had driven most of the Indians back to their homes. The reports of those who returned gave rise to a rumor that the party still out would be, or had been, frozen to death or else attacked and killed. See *New York Herald*, December 23, 1876, p. 6; *ANJ*, December 30, 1876, p. 325. In fact, Captain Randall and the Crows might might well have perished in a severe storm had they not happened upon a small herd of buffalo. They shot some of the animals and thrust their legs into the carcasses for warmth, subsisting for a time on raw meat.

142. By S.O. 140, Military Division of the Missouri, and S.O. 164, DP, the Twenty-third Regiment of Infantry was transferred from the Department of the Platte to the more southerly Department of the Missouri, headquartered at Fort Leavenworth, Kansas (*ANJ*, December 23, 1876, p. 309). The field, staff, and band of the Twenty-third Infantry left Omaha on December 17 and reported to Fort Leavenworth the next day (U.S. Army, Twenty-third Infantry Regimental Returns).

pleased. Crook says that many trails of Indians with travois are passing South towards the Agencies – & he thinks the Campaign at an end. He is waiting for his spies & for his scouts – also for the supplies – but if the first two do not come in in a day or two, or do not report favorably, I think he will return.

We are all satisfied that nothing further can be done, & therefore are all anxious to go back as soon as possible – Were there any hope of striking the hostiles I would say "go on" particularly as we poor Doboys have so far had no show, but if we cant strike there is no sort of use in our staying out here – losing horses & mules, & suffering ourselves without necessity –

A mail came by scout today – but principally papers. I got nothing except one official letter. Had my case filled with whiskey this afternoon, & am now set up. A nice game of whist at night, & got beat. Had a good bath – Weather very threatening – not cold but looks like a bad snow storm – To bed rather late.

December 16, 1876. Belle Fourche

Up late, for camp life. Went over to HdQrs at Court time. Soon disposed of the Lieutenant & afterwards of 3 other cases enlisted men.[143] Adjourned sine die, & told Bourke that if he gave us another case I would sit on him – so I guess we wont have any more. Any quantity of rumors flying about – as regards the forage coming up on the train. In the first place

143. See the journal entry for December 14. Second Lieutenant Otis was judged not guilty of the first charge against him but guilty of the second. He was sentenced to forfeit twenty-five dollars from his next month's pay. The three enlisted men were all found guilty and sentenced to forfeit small amounts from their pay (G.O. 3, December 18, 1876, and G.O. 6, December 21, 1876, PRE Order Book, Bourke Papers). On February 27, 1877, by direction of the president, Second Lieutenant Otis was transferred from the Fourth Cavalry to Battery E of the Fourth Artillery, some of whose units had participated in the Powder River Expedition.

the train is a day or two behind time & it is said that it has no forage – that it will arrive without a pound.[144] We are now entirely out, & if no more is coming we should leave for Ft Fetterman at once. We can't do a thing without forage. If a storm such as may be now expected should now strike us, we may lose from starvation & cold half our stock. If we go in where forage and stabling can be had, every animal will in two months be in condition for another expedition. I must go over tomorw & see the General about our prospects. The day has been cold & blustery, tho not stormy After dark however the long threatened storm set in & it has been snowing fast for some hours. There seems to be a sort of hold up now, but it may be bad or good tomorw. It is getting too late in the season to fool with the weather & I shall urge the Genl to go back at once – unless he has some pretty sure hope of striking a hostile camp or force

December 17, 1876. Belle Fourche

Up late as usual – Went over to Hd Qrs but did not see the Genl. Jordan arrived with a train of 80 wagons – 128,000 lbs forage – 12 days half rations – a paper mail came also, but no letters. Every body in a greater state of doubt than ever as to what will be next move. No president yet!

Trouble with the whiskey mill of course, but have got it on a pretty good basis. Several visitors at night & sat up late.

December 18, 1876. Belle Fourche

Up late as usual – Went over to see Genl Crook in morning. Met Mackenzie there. Had a long & very pleasant visit. There is nothing new. The expected Indians have not arrived & the

144. Contrary to this rumor, General Crook had received notice from the commander of the pack train that it would arrive on December 17 with 128,000 pounds of grain, additional supplies, and a newspaper mail (Bourke diary, December 16, 1876, Bourke Papers). Dodge's entries for December 17 and 18 confirm the accuracy of the information.

Genl is at a stand still. The wagons yesterday brought 1/2 forage for 12 days, & rations to about the 15th Jany. It is said there is another train now nearly due, with 1/2 forage for 10 days more. So with the new outfit our stay in the wilderness is getting more uncertain every day. I thought two days ago that we would probably start on our return for Ft Fetterman by the 20th. Now it is scarcely probable that we will get back there much befor 15 Jany.

If we can do anything I shall be very glad but the prospects are that the hostiles have decamped to beyond where we can reach them, even with our increased stock of supplies Randall <is>was at Ft Reno, at last accounts, with 76 Crow Indians. He is expected daily. No one knows what are the plans of Genl C. I dont believe he has any, but expects to make up his mind when he gets further information. He is a regular bull-dog to hold on, & will not quit unless forced to.

December 19, 1876. Belle Fourche

Up at usual time to find on my breakfast table 4 letters, one from Father, another from Kate Chambless – all containing good news. A courier got in during the night with a bundle of letters & telegrams containing a good deal of news. The political situation is the same. Hayes elected, but as the Dutchman said by a "tam tight squeeze" of a couple of votes, & an impending contest when the votes came to be counted. Brooklyn theatre burned – Horrible catastrophe – Hardee – Inspr. dead – & some small fry resigned or dead[145] But the best news of all is the certainty of my Regt leaving this Dept for

145. Three hundred fifty persons perished in the conflagration that destroyed the Brooklyn Theatre on December 5. Colonel James Hardie, inspector general of the army, died on December 14. The "small fry" Dodge had in mind probably included First Lieutenant Alfred Boyce Bache, Fifth Cavalry, who had been seriously ill during General Crook's summer campaign, remaining with the expedition against medical advice. Lieutenant Bache died on November 12, 1876.

Kansas, or Dept of Platte.[146] Hd Qrs left, or were to leave on 13th. Hinton has gone to Ft Dodge, Haskall to Fort Riley, Smith to Ft Leavenworth. Eskridge is ordered to Gibson – Coppinger & Brady to Reno, (<or>the Arrapahoe agency) Nickerson's Co, Goodale Comdg goes also but I don't know to what post.[147] The three Cos with me Randal Wheaton & Pollock will likely all go to Leavenworth as soon as this Expn is over.[148] I dont know where I will go. My choice Ft Lyon is occupied by a Col. Smith of 19th –[149] I will therefore have most likely Riley Gibson or Dodge I wrote to Bob Williams last night asking him to write to Pope for me, & give me Riley or Gibson as would be better for Tooty.[150] Either would be

146. Dodge meant "Missouri," not "Platte."

147. Company B, under Captain James Henton, was at Fort Dodge, Kansas; Company F, under Captain Joseph T. Haskell, at Fort Riley, Kansas, where Haskell was commanding officer; Company D, under Captain Thomas M. K. Smith, at Fort Leavenworth; Company H, under Captain Richard I. Eskridge, at Fort Gibson, Indian Territory. Company A, under Captain John J. Coppinger, was en route from Fort Hartsuff, Nebraska, to Fort Reno, Indian Territory; Company E, under Captain George K. Brady, from Cheyenne Depot, where Brady had been commanding officer, to Fort Reno, Indian Territory. Company K, under Lieutenant Greenlief A. Goodale in the absence of Captain Azor H. Nickerson, was at Cantonment Reno. Company K left the cantonment on January 8, 1877, and was then ordered to Fort Riley, where it arrived on January 24 and took post.

148. Dodge's prediction was correct. Company C, under Captain Otis W. Pollock; Company G, under Captain Charles Wheaton; and Company I, under Captain George M. Randall, traveled to Fort Leavenworth via Denver and took post there on January 12, 1877.

149. Colonel Charles H. Smith commanded the Nineteenth Infantry, whose headquarters were at this time at Fort Lyon, Colorado. Dodge was familiar with Fort Lyon, having commanded there between October 1869 and February 1871. During that period he had directed the construction of much admired officers' quarters at the post, including a handsome post commander's residence.

150. The three posts where Dodge thought he might be assigned by Brigadier General John Pope, commander of the Department of the Missouri, were Fort Riley, on the Kansas River near Junction City, Kansas; Fort Gibson, on the Republican River near its confluence with the Arkansas and Verdigris Rivers, in Indian Territory; and Fort Dodge, Kansas, on the Arkansas River 370 miles west and south of Fort Leavenworth. Dodge had commanded at Fort Dodge between June 1872 and November 1873.

satisfactory to me, but I want that which suit[s] the health and taste of the "old lady" –

The G. C. M. of which I am President, was ordered to meet again today for trial of a couple of Cavalry Soldiers. Got through with them.[151] We move tomorw a short distance down the river. Am very glad of it, for it is far more tedious lying in Camp, than to make a long march. Dodge read me part of a letter from his wife – about the move. Wrote to Joe & Laura giving directions.[152]

Wrote also to Potter, & a long letter to Father & Mother.

Indians have not arrived & we are all getting decidedly impatient. It is dreadfully irksome to be on such a campaign & doing nothing.

December 20, 1876. Belle Fourche

Reveille at 5.30 a[.m.] – Townsend late – says he got no orders. Broke camp 7. – stopped for nearly an hour at Mackenzies – Genl C. was there. He is mad about his Indians & says that somebody ought to be hung. He will stick it out on this river, until he hears from the Indians. Randal sent a scout to us last night. He will be along in a day or two. But our trouble now is that the expected Indians from the Agencies & the spies, all of whom ought to be here, have not only not arrived but not a word has been heard from them Got into camp before 10 am.

The General is in a terrible humor. The news brought him last night is to the effect that Mason – at Red Cloud – is

151. On this day the general court-martial convened under Dodge on December 14 heard charges against Private John Gorman, Company K, Third Cavalry, and Private Daniel Allman of the same company. The two men were accused of abandoning their posts on guard duty, to the prejudice of good order and military discipline. Both were found guilty and sentenced to forfeit ten dollars of their pay for the next four months, but the sentence of Private Gorman was remitted in view of his previous good character (G.O. 6, December 21, 1876, PRE Order Book, Bourke Papers).

152. The directions no doubt concerned preparations his domestic servants were to make for the move to a new post.

disarming *all* the Indians friendly as well as hostile. Crook's plan is to make a wide & marked distinction between these classes — Those Indians who obey his orders - submit to be counted, & attend all inspections, and whose whereabouts can thus always be known, he allows to keep arms & ponies; those who he cannot rely on, he disarms & dismounts. He thinks that Mason would not dare to go so decidedly against his wishes & plans, unless he had orders to do so from Sheridan.[153] If S. has given the order, it nullifies all that Crook has done, & stops at once any further progress in his plans for the future - This taken with the absence of all information in regard to his spies, has completely knocked the "Old Man" up. He told me that he did not sleep a wink last night, & pretended that he is sick. He is really only worried - I dont blame him for being disgusted. He knows more about the management of Indians than Sheridan will ever know, & it is very hard after working so long & indefatigably to get things in shape, to have all overturned in a moment.

We lie over here tomorw - & there is no telling what effect the news is going to have on the final result of the expn

153. On December 20 General Crook addressed the Indians with his command as follows: "I understand they [the Indians] have been turning in their . . . horses and guns at the Agency. I don't know by what authority. It was not by my order, but I don't know whether it was by orders from Washington or not" (quoted in Bourke diary, December 20, 1876, Bourke Papers). Crook's suspicion that General Sheridan was responsible for the change of policy at Red Cloud Agency was owing in part to the known belief of Sheridan that reliance on Indians for military cooperation and assistance was a dangerous practice. In this case the disarming and dismounting had been ordered by Major Julius W. Mason, Third Cavalry, in command at Camp Robinson, with the tacit approval of Sheridan. On December 3, 1876, Mason reported to Sheridan that he had collected from the Indians at Red Cloud Agency 290 ponies and 75 guns, chiefly breechloaders, and expected to complete the disarming within a few days. "I do not anticipate any further trouble here," he wrote, "the Indians being harmless by want of arms and ponies and disposed to do what is right" (Sioux War Special File). The Omaha *Bee* for December 27, 1876, reported that H. C. Dear, post trader at Camp Canby near Red Cloud Agency, had identified Major Mason as initiator of the "experiment" with the Indians, "which is proving a great success" (clipping in Bourke diary No. 17, Bourke Papers).

Snow last night, but lovely clear & bright today. Distance 6. miles.

Frank White, Chief of Pawnees came over to call on me this afternoon & brought me a small portion of the scalp of Dull Knife's youngest son, who was killed by the Pawnees in the affair of Mackenzie.[154] It is the very greatest compliment (in his estimation) that he could pay me, & almost makes us brothers. I went over to the Pawnee Camp at night & paid a visit to Maj North. He says the Sioux yesterday gave the Pawnees a grand begging dance, in which the latter were badly fleeced, it being regarded as a mark of great meanness not to give something on such occasions. The wily Sioux secured 50 or 60 horses & a great many other valuable things. Frank gave 3 horses & a suit of finery. North gave some interesting facts in regard to the Pawnee religion. They believe in one God, from whom comes all good & all bad. They are fatalists & accept everything as <h>His will without murmur or cavil. They are very religious – have no oaths in their Language never take the name of the Deity in vain. Offer sacrifices, & set aside certain things as consecrated to Him.[155]

Some old plug of a horse will be offered to the Gt. Spirit by some devout individual. After that the horse is taken the best care of, is never ridden nor even bridled, never struck by a whip, & is regarded as sacred by all In ceremonial smokes they emit two puffs upward to the Great Spirit, & one downward to the earth, which is called the "Father of the dead." They do not believe in a Bad God, or Devil. They are excessively filthy personally – but have more regard to what we call the decencies of life than the Cheyennes. They are more careful of the exposure of their persons, & do not sell the persons of their wives.

154. The *New York Herald*, December 1, 1876, p. 3, reported that three sons of Dull Knife had died in the battle against Colonel Mackenzie.

155. The religious beliefs of Native Americans of the plains were a topic of particular interest to Dodge. He had included several chapters on the subject in his book; see, for example, PNA, pp. 247–62.

Men & women are all loose if opportunity serves, but take great pains not to be caught – They are extremely superstitious, & most of their actions are determined by signs & omens.

Frank says they never wish to go on the war path again, but to go to farming & raising stock[156]

December 21, 1876. Belle Fourche

A bad storm came on in the night with snow & wind. Very cold. My stove pipe would not draw, & I was waked up by a tent so full of smoke that I could not see across it. My man is a first class Dutchman willing & obedient, but *so* stupid. He has never yet been able to learn how to make a fire in a Sibley stove,[157] – the easiest managed stove if one understands it, the most refractory if one does'nt. Got up late & had a chilly uncomfortable breakfast. A Drunken Cavalryman frozen last night.

Many visitors in the morning, all anxious to know what we are going to do – to which conundrum there is no answer – It now appears that the train which was to bring us supplies has gone on to Reno, & left the supplies there. We have now only to 2d Jany, & must decide on something very soon.

Having written this much I strolled over to Hd Qrs. Saw the Genl a moment but he looked so disconsolate & preoccupied that I had not the courage to tackle him. Went into Bourkes tent & gassed with him for some time, then started to go to my tent. On the road I met Mackenzie just coming in to Camp, told him that C. was down in the mouth & that he had better come over to my tent – "That is the more reason for our going to see him" said he. ["]Lets go & give him some consolation & propose a game of whist." I could hardly keep from smiling

156. This had been the main theme of Frank White in his talk at the council with General Crook on November 19. Bourke recorded the speech almost verbatim in his diary entry for that day (Bourke Papers); see also the summary in Bourke, *Mackenzie's Last Fight with the Cheyennes*, p. 10.

157. Named after its inventor, Henry Hopkins Sibley, this stove consisted of a single cone of sheet iron with a stovepipe at its apex, the whole resting on a grate at ground level.

at this for they were almost the identical words used by Crook to me when I told him how downhearted Mackenzie was after his fight – Of course I agreed & we went in to the Genl's tent. After the first greetings Mac proposed the game. "I can't play today," said the old man. "I have got to have a big Indian Council today & it is nearly time. The fact is," continued he after a pause "I have made up my mind to turn back tomorw & want to give the Indians a good talk & let them go direct to their Res[ervatio]n" He then went on to tell us of the difficulties which beset him – the apperent impossibility of finding out exactly where the hostile camp is, the failure of his spies to report, proving that the position of that camp is very distant from us – the folly of attempting to scout in search of it in the vast country in which the hostiles roam in our depleted condition as to rations & forage – & with our animals so reduced in flesh & strength.

Mackenzie & I both agreed with him, both asserted our willingness to stick as long as there was a hope – but that hope being now past the first consideration was our men & animals. Mac said it was not his responsibility but that he had thought for a week past that it would be best to return. I said that I would probably gain more by a successful campaign than either of them & that my disposition was to stick as long as there was a chance – That as it was now conceded there was no chance I thought the best thing to do was to put the men & animals in good quarters as soon as possible. They were not so much run down now, but that two months of care & good feed would not put them in condition to take the field again – while if he waited until they were quite broken down he would not only lose many, but the others would not be recuperated in time for a Campaign next spring.

So after an hours talk I came away to give the order for the move to the rear –[158] The Indians went up to Hd Qrs soon

158. On December 21 General Crook sent a telegram to Fort Fetterman for dispatch to General Sheridan at Chicago, reporting his decision to return to the fort. "The worn out condition of all the citizen and Army transportation in this part of the country, makes it impossible to keep this Command in the

after, were talked to, & are to start tomorw for Red Cloud. They are very jolly & have been dancing singing & tom-toming ever since I dont believe there is a man in the Comd, who is not happier for the order.

I wrote several letters to go by the courier, & sent those I had previously written – Tooty, Father & Mother, Kate Chambless, Bob Williams, Potter & Joe and Laura. I had already written one to Father & Mother so wrote another with the good news.

Mackenzie came in just after dinner & we had a good talk. He is annoyed that he did not do better with the chance he had, yet pleased that he did so well, & that we all commend him.

Campbell visited me at night & we had an "Old Army" talk – scandal reminiscence anecdote & stories of all kinds very badly mixed with sundry drinks of whiskey. The *order* to move to the rear did not come until after tattoo. Been snowing all day & getting worse tonight.

Friday, December 22, 1876. Belle Fourche

I started on this expedition on Friday. I start on my return on Friday. My little wife would be worried at such flying in the face of the Ancient Superstition[159] but Friday has always been a very lucky day to me except in minor discomforts

Reveille at 5.30. Broke camp at 7.10. It was snowing when we started, but by 9 Oclk held up, & tried to be good. Could'nt make it however, & soon after got worse rapidly – By 11 am

---

Field any longer," he wrote. Crook first estimated that the return to Fort Fetterman would require eight days, but changed that number to six (PRE Order Book, p. 90, Bourke Papers; Sioux War Special File).

159. Friday has traditionally been considered the day when Adam was created, when he and Eve were expelled from Paradise, when he repented, when he died, when Christ was crucified, and when the dead will rise for the Last Judgment. To the superstitious, Friday was not an auspicious day to begin any doubtful undertaking.

we were enjoying a most terrific norther – snow wind & cold combined. I halted my comd every little while & made them wait the arrival of our wagons for I have no notion of a seperation from those useful receptacles in such weather. About 1 pm I overtook Genl Crook – ensconced in a nook under high bluffs – & here the camp was made. The road was terribly bad. Some bad crossings & steep pitches – but bad even at the best places, from being covered with ice, which made the frozen ground as difficult to get footing on as the smoothest sheet of ice. Every little pitch had to be dug down, not because it was too steep, but simply to give footing to the mules. In some places the road had to be picked & cut with axes for many yards. By 4 p.m. the wagons of my Comd were all in. Genl C. had selected the site for his Hd Qr tents – gave me a very small space for my Comd – and apparently overlooked a sweet little cove just at the foot of a high bluff bank with trees & bushes all around. I siezed upon that immediately for my Hd Qrs – & have the very best position of all. While waiting for the wagons we put out a thermometer & found that it indicated 5° This was in our little sheltered nook. I have no doubt that twas at least –5° on the plain on top of the bluff, over which we had just come. Several of the Officers & men had their noses & ears frozen. Altogether it has been anything but a lovely day & if we had to face the storm instead of going before it, we must have lost many men. I did not suffer very greatly though several times I thought I ought to stop & don my leggins and other storm-defiers – but I stuck it out. My fingers & toes suffered, but I got to camp all right. The ther[momete]r went down to 0 about 6 pm but after that it moderated a little. It is now 9 pm, – about 5° & snowing quite fast. There is every prospect of a similar day tomorw, for which I propose to be better prepared. We are rather short of wood tonight but for at least two camps ahead there is none. We must take from here enough to keep us from freezing. This is the 2d day of the storm. Tomorw ought to be the last. I am truly glad we are going back, for such weather must have broken up our organization & killed off our animals in a few days more –

I have been summing up today some of the causes of Crooks failure. I find on calculation that our transpn ought to carry 60 days rations for the whole Comd. Give 2 wagons to each Compy & carry besides 50 days' half forage for the animals. Why it did not I have discovered. The Qr Mr Dept. – Wagon Masters Teamsters &c – carry bedding enough for 40 companies, wall tents for 50 companies, Sibley stoves for 20 companies, & 44 cooking stoves, of which there are only 2 others in the whole Comd – Genl C's mess and Major Townsend's mess In other words the Citizen employees of the QM Dept carry more impedimenta than would be required by a force of troops nearly double that we have. There are 27 Cos troops including the Co Hd Qr G[uar]d. These Citizens carry the baggage of at least 45 Comps. Besides this the Citizens are held in no sort of discipline & do just as they please. Our mules are broken down not so much by their work, as by positive neglect. The teamsters tie the mules to the wagon tongue when they get into camp, put some corn in the food trough & some Cotton wood under the tongue, then go off to their tents with the supply train. In the morning they get to their teams barely in time to hitch up & pull out & the mules get nothing to eat in the morning. Yet Genl C. insists that Fury is a most excellent Qr Mr & that he could not get along without him. Crooks great lack is organization. He knows nothing about it & is obliged to trust to others. He asks no questions & believes what is said to him. He gives no orders – examines into no details. He is told he can carry only certain stores & does his best on that. He thinks his mules break down from hard work when they are neglected & starved. His successes must always be accidents as was this last – & he must fail – because he cannot himself organize, & has not the judgment to select men who can. He is brave tenacious & the best judge of Indian character in the Army, but he lacks — Distance today 13 miles.[160]

160. On the pages that follow, Dodge wrote several entries that are not reproduced here. On p. [81V] is a list of "Camps & Distances of March from Crazy Woman," with a column that shows a running sum that begins with the 256 miles marched from Medicine Bow to Cantonment Reno and accumulates from that point. On p. [82R], written with the notebook reversed, is a list of mileages from Sidney, Nebraska, to Red Cloud Agency. On page [82V] is a tabulation of the same mileages in reverse order. Following this page, on the inside back cover, Dodge sketched a map; see the entry for December 6.

Journal Three: December 23, 1876– January 8, 1877

Powder River
Expedition
Winter
1876
No 3 –[161]

December 23, 1876. Belle Fourche, Camp 7

If I have boasted that the hardships of a winter campaign were bearable I apologize. The ther[mometer] went down very low in the night & at 7<30> am was at 0. Reveille at 6.30, broke camp about 7.45. A bad crossing of the Creek just in our front delayed everything I myself left camp about 8.30 & not a single one of our wagons had yet succeeded in crossing – I was satisfied that some of them would not get over before 12 m.

a crossing

Half a mile further on was <one> ^ equally bad, & a mile on, still another. I felt that the safe crossing of the three could not be effected before 1 or 2 pm – so I put out after my Comd

161. This manuscript journal consists of seventy-five unnumbered pages in a copy of "Pocket Scratch Book No. 4," a stiff cardboard pad measuring 3 3/8 x 4 7/8 inches, to which are attached sheets of plain unlined paper. Although the pad is designed to permit easy ripping away of its individual slips, in this case all the pages are present. On the bottom side of the cardboard pad Dodge wrote in black ink, "Winter Campaign [/] 1876." Except as noted here, the journal is written entirely in pencil. Pages [1V], [2], [71]–[74], and [75R] are blank. The text begins on p. [1R]; at the bottom right of that page "7.57" is written upside down.

to prevent its getting too far away from the wagons. I overtook it 3 miles ahead, ensconced in a ravine, & with fires built. I joined them & we remained there until 12 m, when the train began to appear in good shape. We pushed on, & found Genl Crook & the Cavy on the Creek about 8 miles above our old camp, or eleven miles from our camp of last night. The wagons commenced to arrive by 3 pm & by 5 all mine were in The supply train did not all arrive until about dark. The difficulties are manifold. Only two weeks ago we went over this same ground 20 miles a day. Then our mules were comparatively fresh & strong. There was little or no snow, and the ground was soft & gave a foothold. Now the mules are weak & poor & have little food, they are smooth shod, the ground is not only covered with snow, but is frozen as hard as iron & with the snow and ice on it it is slippery as glass. The mules can gain no footing to pull up & even a small hill has to be cut or dug to give a foothold for them. This has been a day of terrible hardship & trial for all of us – men & animals. It cleared off about noon, the sun came out & the wind shifted to the south – but all to no good purpose. The ther[momete]r has been between 2° & –2° all day. It has been bitter in the extreme & well wrapped as I was, I had trouble to keep my fingers & nose from freezing. My Ku Klux cap disappeared in the most mysterious manner this morning, & I find it very difficult to protect my face without it.

We have very little wood & that the poorest kind, and we shook & shivered in our tents until dinner, about 7 pm – after which I went to bed to keep warm.

General C. talks of attempting a short cut from some point on this stream to Wind Creek. His object is to make a road across there. It will be useful hereafter. I have talked against this plan as it is no weather in which to make experiments, & he might get the Comd involved in the bad lands & lose every man.

It is a terribly cold night & getting colder every moment. It must be 5 to 6 below 0 now. There was a large & very brilliant rainbow around the sun for 3 or 4 hours today. It is called a Sun-dog & portends cold and stormy weather.[162] It is fine weather for campaigning & tent life is a romance No one frozen today which is a wonder. No wood – Distance 11. miles.

December 24, 1876. Belle Fourche

Reveille at 6.30. The mules were herded last night, that is the teamsters turned them loose, & they went where they pleased – consequently when my wagons were loaded there was no team to pull them. However the teamsters fussed around & so got their mules together that Townsend was able to get off at 10 a.m. – I had started long before. The road was good, but smooth as ice, & the mules had a hard time. I got into Camp at 1 p.m. The Cavy ahead of me as usual – by 3 pm all the wagons were in in good shape though several mules were abandoned – Our Camp is the same as No 1 on the Belle Fourche –[163] or at the water nearest the head & Camped in the same place, a deep ravine, and the Comd is in its old place. The day has been terrific. My Ther[momete]r only indicated −17°. At 7 <am> this morning the mercury was in the bulb, several degrees below [−]17°, & I am of the opinion that during the night the temperature was well nigh −30. I am led to this conclusion by the fact that the coldest time of the night was about 12 – after that it moderated perceptibly. Yet so late as 7, it was −17, & all the degrees between that indicated and the bulb – at least 4 or 5 possibly more. I think the temperature at 7 am was about −20. I am sure it had been 10° lower in the middle of the night.

162. In *Our Wild Indians* Dodge wrote that the "Arctic phenomena" seen on this winter campaign included "magnificent Aurora Borealis, 'sun-dogs,' or the appearance of five Suns, and the beautiful 'bridal veil,' every particle of moisture in the atmosphere being congealed in tiny particles, so that when the sun shone upon it, everything was seen as through a silver veil" (p. 507). See the journal entry for December 29.

163. This was the camp of December 7.

It has been a bright sunshiny day – the sun being warm enough to be perceptible & occasion remark. Yet the temperature during the whole day has not been higher than –10°. Fortunately there has been very little wind – one can stand still cold – but I have never worked harder than I did today in keeping my nose & fingers from freezing. I this am put on my buckskins and have not been uncomfortable except my face & my hands – but I really feared I would freeze some part of me.[164]

Soon after getting in camp my striker[165] – Kistler – came running up with my cap, which he said he had found in my bed. Now as I went through each separate item of that bed twice since that cap was lost without finding it, I am constrained to suspect that some one gobbled that cap, but brought it back when he found I made such a fuss about its loss However, I won't growl. I have got the cap, & my nose is pretty safe in the future – While I was at dinner I got a message from Genl Crook saying he would like to see me in half an hour – but in such terms as led me to believe the request social instead of official – I went, of course, but Genl C's tent having no light, I went into Bourke's, where I found Randall, just in from his extraordinary trip in search of the Crows[166]

He brought in about 80 – too late to be of service, & they can only go back. He is looking well considering the hardships he has gone through. After a chat with him I went to the Genls tent & soon after Mackenzie & Townsend came in – all by invitation. After a little while the "swarry"[167] was brought in, consisting of a <most> pitcher of most excellent brandy

164. Dodge refers to his buckskin drawers. See the entry for November 29.

165. A term then in common use to designate a soldier-servant.

166. Captain Randall and his contingent of Crow warriors reached the camp of General Crook at about 6 P.M. on this day. The Indians set out on their trip home on December 26.

167. A humorous term for an evening's entertainment, after *soirée*. The earliest example of its use cited in the *Oxford English Dictionary* is from Dickens's *Pickwick Papers* (1837).

George M. Randall, c. 1895 (Courtesy of Paul L. Hedren)

punch *hot*. We all did ample justice to it & the occasion, drinking to the occasion & to our absent loved ones – & happy meetings with them. Randal brought me a letter from Goodale & several telegrams to Genl C. We meet a train tomorw with rations & forage – another waits us at Wind Creek. We had a jolly evening, drinking & telling stories – but alas! the pitcher was not the widows cruise[168] & when the Genl went out to replenish, he found that there was no more. The staff had gobbled all.[169] The Staff is a nuisance & ought to be abolished. Of course with nothing to drink we soon broke up. I came home to find all my people in bed – & no fire in my tent. I soon had one however for I had plenty of wood. When I got into camp I found that my Sergt had deceived me saying we had plenty of wood, when we had not, & I was in the hapless condition. No wood, & no chance to get any without genius. Egan had lots of wood – enough for Hd Qrs and to spare. I went up there. He was hard at work pitching Hd Qr tents. He looked cold and thirsty. I invited him to come to my tent & get a drink, and he at once accepted. We went casually by his wood pile. I told him I was out of wood, & that I would like a log. In the openness of his heart, he told me to send up a man & he would give me one. I did so – you bet – & have a fire A drink is worth a log of wood any day — The weather has moderated greatly, but it is still far below zero. There is however no wind & we have every prospect of a good day tomorw. I hope so most cordially. No water, no grass no wood tonight – & yet it is Xmas Eve. How different for some people – Only <8>7 miles today.

168. The story of Elijah and the widow's cruse, which miraculously refilled itself, is in 1 Kings 17:12–16.

169. Apparently the culprits were Captains Egan and Furey, who together had mixed the punch, and General Crook's personal staff, First Lieutenants Schuyler and Bourke (Bourke diary, Bourke Papers). Bourke claimed in *On the Border with Crook* that Crook "never indulged in stimulant of any kind" (109); however, the general seems to have made an exception on this occasion.

December 25, 1876. Near Grand Spring

Was waked up about 3. am by the cold, & though I had so much covering that it was cumbersome from its weight I could not get warm. Tried all manner of ways, and finally was rejoiced to hear reveille. Waited for some time for my man to come & make my fire, & getting impatient looked out to find it[170] still dark night. It was Mackenzie's reveille I had heard, & I had to wait & shiver for an hour & a half until my reveille should bring my man. At last both came. I had last night, in anticipation of the terrible cold, cut a lot of small shavings to kindle the fire, & showed them to my man. He is however a German – one of the most incapable of that incapable nation – & with all my previous instructions – the daily making of fire for near two months – & the pine splinters, he utterly failed, & after seeing him bungle unsuccessfully for full 20 minutes, I was at last obliged to get up in my night clothes & make the fire myself. My preparations were fortunately so complete that it took me not three minutes, or I must have frozen. It was intensely, terrifically cold. At 7 am the thermometer was frozen – the mercury rather. The Doctor thawed it out but in half an hour afterwards it was frozen again hard. It must have been 50° below zero. Everything & everybody was frozen up. Breakfast was frozen stiff before it could be set on the table. Fortunately we got hot coffee. When all the wagons were loaded, it was found that the teamsters had not reported, & when they at last came to their teams, many mules were absent) had to be hunted up. It was at least 10 oclock am before the teams were ready to start. I do not understand how so usually astute a man as Genl Crook, can be so utterly obtuse as to the value and capacity of his Qr Mr The whole Comd delayed at least 3 hours in the morning, because a few of his teamsters chose to sleep a little longer – & yet he appears to think it all right.

170. Dodge wrote "in."

I started about 9 a.m, leaving my comd to follow. The road is generally good, but there are two terribly bad places. I got into camp about 2 pm reported and got my camp ground. The wagons commenced to get in by 4, but all were not in until between 7 & 8 p.m. Men & wagons kept standing waiting, without food for more than 14 hours – all to enable some teamsters – princes in disguise – to sleep a little longer in the morning I ventilated my opinion on such arrangements very openly. The General listened only half a minute, then
went
<ran> ^ away. The staff had to listen, & Fury's chief clerk attempted to defend Fury's action by saying that if he discharged one teamster a hundred would leave. "Let them go at once" I said. "I will give you a hundred better teamsters in an hour." The fact is Fury is entirely under the Control of these men – He is afraid of them – They know it, & do just as they please. Mackenzie tried to mollify me tonight by saying that Fury was doing his best & was really a very good specimen of a regular Qr Mr. I agreed with him entirely. I do think Fury a willing, energetic, hard working man, & one of the best regular Qr Mrs I know, but he is utterly unfit to have charge of such a train as this. Nor do I know any regular Qr Mr who is. I do know several Lieutenants of the Line who would run it perfectly. Lawton, Mackenzie's Qr Mr,[171] could do it well, & Trout would have the whole thing run as smoothly as a Sewing

171. By "Lieutenants of the Line" Dodge means officers not serving as members of the Quartermaster Corps but performing the duties of a quartermaster while attached to units of the infantry, cavalry, or artillery. First Lieutenant Henry W. Lawton, regimental quartermaster of the Fourth Cavalry, served on the Powder River Expedition as quartermaster of the cavalry brigade under Colonel Mackenzie. Lawton had served under Mackenzie as quartermaster and commissary officer for several years and knew his business well. According to Charles M. Robinson, he was "a superb organizer with a talent for getting things done and no patience for red tape" (*Bad Hand*, p. 87; a photograph of Lawton is on p. 88).

machine –[172] I am utterly and thoroughly disgusted with the management of the Logistics of this Campaign. There is no use saying anything and it only makes enemies. I have said more than enough to record my protest against such management, & as it is of no avail, I congratulate myself that the expedition is over, & I most sincerely hope I will never go on another under Crook – As I have before said, he is entirely deficient in organization, & organization is necessary, not only to success, but to the health & comfort of the Troops.

The March was a very trying one. When we started the mercury was frozen, but it moderated very rapidly, getting to about zero by 1 p.m. Getting through the pass of Pumpkin Buttes was like going into another climate. On the other side I was frozen up, & bundled up. As soon as we passed, I got off my Kuklux Cap, & was even too hot at that. Everything is comparative, & zero is warm & comfortable after 50 below. Tonight 9.30 pm, the Thir[mometer] is 12° above – & I am lying on the outside of my bed writing this, – quite comfortable in a temperature that would be considered very cold in the east. Took dinner with Mackenzie tonight my teams getting in after the dinner was over. He came to my tent afterwards & spent a half hour. I was at his tent when <th>my troops came in, & though I took the pains to come out & instruct

172. The versatile and energetic First Lieutenant John F. Trout, Company B, Twenty-third Infantry, who was serving at this time as post adjutant at Fort Dodge, Kansas, was Dodge's beau ideal of a quartermaster. During 1872 and 1873 Trout had participated in construction of a military telegraph line from San Diego, California, to posts in Arizona. In 1874 and 1875 he had played a key role in distributing emergency supplies to citizens in Nebraska and Kansas whose crops were devastated by grasshoppers. In the latter year he had also performed with great credit under Dodge as quartermaster of the Black Hills Expedition; see Dodge, ***Black Hills Journals***, pp. 44, 72, 107, 134, 185, 197, and passim. Dodge again secured the assistance of Lieutenant Trout in 1879, when he established a new post in Indian Territory, Cantonment North Fork Canadian River. However, in consequence of a serious injury Trout had sustained during the Black Hills expedition, in July 1879 a medical board found him unfit for active service and granted him an indefinite leave of absence. He retired from the army in 1883.

Townsend where to go, he as usual botched everything & got his wagons, tents & cook fires just into my Hd. Qrs. I'll locate him hereafter. Take it all in all it is a Xmas long to be remembered, & I don't care ever to have another like it. Excellent Camp. Wood & water plenty & good grass. 3 horses & 3 mules killed or abandoned today. Distance 20 miles –

December 26, 1876.
Camp on Mini Pusa[173] near mouth of Wind Creek

Reveille at 6.30, but late getting off again on account of the tardiness of teamsters. Genl C. sent me word early to follow his trail, as he proposed to strike out a new road. I did so. We had to cross a few bad ravines but the <road> route was good. Our course was almost directly south – varying a very little to the eastward, & in about 10 miles we struck the regular beaten road, (that from Fetterman to Reno, & by which we came out) It was like an old friend, & all hailed it with satisfaction. After about 16 miles we struck Wind Creek where we camped going north –[174] There being no wood & the water being frozen solid, we came down Wind Ck nearly a mile to its junction with the middle fork of the south fork of Cheyenne. It is an immense bed with plenty of timber, but no running water. However we found a few water holes, the ice on them being a foot thick – & cut a way into them with axes. The water is abominable full of alkaline impurities The water at Grand Spring last night made me sick & this tonight caps the climax. I should mention as one of the minor discomforts of a campaign in this country, that with the single exception of Willow Creek – (where we camped <th> on our night march after the Indians)[175] we have not found a drop of palatable water.

173. "Dry Water," the Indian name for a branch of the Cheyenne River later known as Muggins Fork.

174. This was on November 16.

175. Dodge wrote "Indains." His command had bivouacked on Willow Creek on November 26.

It is all saturated with Gypsum, or other alkaline matter, & is not only sweet and sickish to the taste, but acts violently on the bowels, bringing on griping pains & profuse foetid discharges. I have suffered all day, but have gotten "kinder" used to it. Another of our common discomforts is the snow. For more than a month, we have been marching, living & sleeping in the snow, until we have almost come to regard it as a natural covering of the earth. I have the loose snow scraped off the ground inside of my tent – but make no effort to have it cleaned away This would require too much work. In fact the whole tent floor would have to be dug up – no easy matter when the ground is frozen for a foot in depth. We cant drive a tent pin. A hole is first made in the frozen soil with a pick, & the pin inserted. The snow just around the stove melts & becomes a mud puddle. I have a couple of grain sacks beside my bed which serve as rug, & prevent the ground underneath from thawing & getting damp – Under my bed & table the snow is always intact when I leave the spot in the morning.

Another & great discomfort in so cold a country is the scarcity of fuel. We always go to wood if possible, but many times we cant find it. Last night we were lucky enough to get an abundance & expecting none at Wind Creek where we camped going out, we brought some with us. By coming down Wind Creek to its junction with this branch (called Middle Fork) we find a great abundance.

Another minor trouble is the scarcity of water. Even when we camp at water holes, the supply is <more> frequently so limited that we cant wash our faces in the morning, & I have for
quit
some time ^ expecting more than one wash of my hands in a day. So we are jolly dirty – but dont mind it a bit. It is really astonishing to see how comfortable pleasant & jovial men can be, living as we do.

Yesterday while at dinner with Mackenzie he was remarking on the general success of our campaign, and "We are now going back" said he "without any suffering at all". "Well" I said, "while I agree with you generally on the good effect of our winters work, I can not agree that we have done it without suffering. We have not suffered permanent ill, nor lost our lives or our limbs, but when a man lies in his bed under a weight of clothing actually uncomfortable, & yet shakes & trembles with cold – when he has to work with his nose & his fingers for three or four hours without intermission to prevent their freezing, he suffers, & he suffers acutely. It is nothing to boast of, when a man has a good heart, & accepts what fate sends him, – but did he give up, he would suffer permanently. One additional step, would have made our suffering permanent for some of us. So while we congratulate ourselves in getting through without permanent disability, we cannot say truly that we have done so without suffering." "Well," he replied laughing, ["]I mean we have not suffered like many other poor fellows under similar circumstances – Henry's Command for instance."[176] No man or men can go through a winter campaign in this country, without great suffering – bodily torture – & if he has the pluck and manliness to go through it without complaint or murmur, it is only a proof of those qualities, & not that he is comfortable. Every man of this Comd has suffered acutely, yet one hears no complaint.

Yesterday morning a man was striking a tent, & without thinking picked up a number of iron tent pins carried them to the bag in which they were to be put & threw them down. They took with them all the skin of the inside of his hand.

Some of the feed troughs furnished by the Qr Mrs Dept are of iron – All that I noticed since this cold snap are covered

176. Colonel Mackenzie was referring to the almost disastrous scouting party, under Captain Guy V. Henry, Third Cavalry, from Camp Robinson into the Black Hills in December 1874–January 1875. The command had suffered greatly from severe winter conditions in the course of its unsuccessful search for U.S. citizens trespassing in the region.

with blood & pieces of flesh where the poor mules have got their lips or tongues in contact with the iron while eating –

We found here waiting for us a train loaded with forage & all the Animals have tonight a good Xmas supper.[177]

There was also a large mail for our Command. I got a letter from Father & Mother dated 5th – all well – a little scared, but jolly. Wishing the boy to distinguish himself, but hoping he will get into no danger – just such a contradictory letter as a Dear old Dad and Mom would write to their only Boybaby – It did me a world of good, & reconciled me somewhat to going home without any special glory. The world applauds success, while success is an accident that may come to the stupid & unenergetic, as well as to the brightest & hardest worker. The world applauds the success, but conscience approves him, who does his work to the best of his ability whether he be successful or not. Neither myself nor my comd have done anything brilliant but we have done our very best, & had our luck put us in a fight, we would have made a name for ourselves – or I am mightily mistaken. Thats all!

The order for my Reg[imen]t to go to Kansas, is a fixed fact – Letter from Rice – Hd Qrs left on 16th.[178] Thats good. No letter from Julia. The poor little woman thinks she writes every week. Father & Mother write every week, & I get letters regularly by every mail. I cant blame her for letter writing is her purgatory – & she takes more time & trouble in writing one letter, than a hundred would cost me. The weather today

177. On December 21 General Crook had sent a message by courier to the commanding officer at Cantonment Reno that the expedition would arrive at the camp on Wind Creek on December 25. Any wagon train then en route to the command was to set its course toward the camp at Wind Creek and wait there. If no such train was yet on the trail, one was to leave the cantonment at once, carrying to the camp a supply of rations for two full days, or about 56,000 pounds (PRE Order Book, pp. 91–92, Bourke Papers).

178. First Lieutenant William F. Rice, quartermaster of the Twenty-third Infantry, was reporting the relocation of that unit's headquarters to Fort Leavenworth.

has been delightful. Ther[momete]r from 12° this am. to 22° at 2 pm – a lovely temperature – & springlike after the experience of the last few days

Excellent camp – water bad & scarce, but we are sheltered & have plenty of wood. Distance 17 miles

December 27, 1876. South Fork, Mini Pusa

Had to make my own fire again this a.m. My man is wretchedly stupid but tries so hard that I have not the heart to get rid of him. The troops got off at 7.30. I remained behind to see my wagons packed. We were all late with our breakfast & my wagons were the very last to leave Camp. It was snowing hard, & kept it up all day, a regular Norther. Fortunately it struck us in rear – & bad as was the day we did not suffer much, as it was not extremely cold. The Ther[momete]r was however not far above zero. One man had his nose badly frosted.

A rascally Doboy came near making a vacancy for some body, for in shooting at a rabbit, his ball which missed the rabbit, of course, passed apparently directly through my party, & so near that my horse dodged & shook his head. It was a long tedious ride. The men bolled[179] along splendidly. I soon overtook the column & came on ahead. I got to camp 2 p.m., the troops abt 3 & the wagons kept coming for an hour later. Everything was in by a little after 4 pm After getting things started for a comfortable night I went over to see Genl Crook. He leaves us tomorw to go in to Fetterman – we take two days to make the distance

I spoke to him about our going to Kansas, that we had a long journey ahead, & that it would be a favor if he would allow us to go on at once. He said he did not intend to issue orders breaking up the expedition but would issue special orders

179. This is Dodge's unusual spelling of "bowled," which recurs in the entry for January 4.

relieving me from duty with it. I then asked him to order us all to Omaha – to which he demurred, & had various extra ways of doing a very simple thing. Wanted me to order the Captains & 1st Sergts of Cos to Omaha to get all the property, &c &c. He totally ignores the fact that all of us have houses fitted up at Omaha Bks & that it takes a little time to pack up. However I don't doubt but I will get every thing all right – with or without his consent –

A large paper mail with a few letters came today, from somewhere. I got a letter from Laura – all is in good condition at home – as she says <Ebery> "Everything is getting on splendidly & the cow has a calf"

My tent full of visitors until 10. p.m. Had a very pleasant evening. Campbell sent me the Army & Navy Journal, which has a good notice of my book – which however is not out yet – <not> or was not when the notice was written –[180]

It is not snowing at present & we may have a good day tomorw. First rate camp, plenty of wood & water – grass scarce as Cavy camped here going up. Distance 21 miles —

December 28, 1876. Sage Creek, First Crossing

Had to make my own fire again this a.m. D—d my stryker a little for his stupidity when he commenced to whimper – whereat my easy soul relented, & I felt bad. I am too good tempered. I feel it more & more every day. Everybody in contact with me takes advantage of it. My cook swindles & steals from me – My tent pins are stolen – my fire is not made – yet I "bear the ills I have, rather than fly to others I know not of" —[181] I begin to think I am getting too old &

180. An anonymous prepublication notice of *The Plains of the Great West* appeared in *ANJ*, December 2, 1876, p. 269. The published work was reviewed in *ANJ*, January 20, 1877, p. 378. Extracts from the book appeared in the issues of January 27, 1877, p. 389, and February 3, 1877, p. 411.

181. An adaptation of lines from the "To be, or not to be" soliloquy in *Hamlet*, III.i.81–82.

philosophical to do very well for myself. When little things go wrong I find myself constantly saying "is it worth the trouble of a row –" & I generally decide in the negative – & this is wrong, for it is the little things that make life, & if we attend to the little things as they occur we will generally have an occasion to attend to greater things. What with laziness & force of habit, I dont attend to the little things & though I can moralize over my failure tonight I wont do any better tomorw.

I stopped just here to put some wood in my stove & while doing so Dr Price came to my tent to tell me that the thermometer indicates 15° below zero – & I am rather disposed to think that moralizing at that temperature, & in a tent, is rather an unusual thing –

It has been cold all day. When we started 7.45 am it was snowing a little – very fine icy pellets. It stopped that and kept getting colder. On the march the temperature was from 6 to 10° above, but after sunset it became much colder. It will probably be 25° below zero before morning. It is astonishing what low temperatures we get to endure without knowing it. At no time so far this winter have I had on all the trappings I have provided – nor have I so far worn an under coat – nor felt the need of one. I have on a perfect bundle of clothing – two flannel & 1 buckskin shirt, a vest, a cardigan & an overcoat – one pair of flannel <&> one pair buckskin drawers & a pair of soldier pants protect my legs Two pairs woollen socks, a pair of soldier boots & buffalo overshoes keep my feet warm. My head boasts a Ku Klux cap with visor to cover my face – a thick padded woollen hood – over which is tied a cashmere handkerchief. On my hands are a pair of silk & a pair of woollen gloves – (I have sealskin but they are very cold) This is my day gear for very cold days, & I have worn
all
it ∧ but a few times. Besides these I have a thick undercoat, a pair of Llama leggins, & a water & air proof overcoat which I have not worn. I am now lying in bed covered with a couple

of blankets, but with arms & shoulders exposed. I have a stove & tolerable fire, but it is almost incredible to think I can be so comfortable in a tent, with the temperature outside as low as it is – Weather that our eastern friends would think unbearable, we find very comfortable – Think of riding for seven hours with the Ther[momete]r below zero & think of sleeping in a tent without fire with the ther[momete]r 50° below zero. We have had it at least that – though we could not tell exactly how low the temperature was, as mercury freezes at 42° below. On the night before Xmas we went to bed with the ther[momete]r –30. When we got up the mercury was frozen One of the officers thawed it out, hung up the ther[momete]r, & in two minutes it was again frozen. This was repeated & it took longer to thaw the mercury over the fire, than it did to freeze it when the instrument was hung out. There's weather –

Genl Crook left us this am & went into Fetterman.[182] We came on quietly & slowly. The troops arrived at this camping place about 3 pm. The road is fairly good, but the marching is bad – the snow & sand clogging & balling the feet. The Comd was pretty well played out when we got here, but there was very little straggling. Townsend has no discretion about marching the men, & rushed them at a great rate today He was excited I suppose by the prospect of soon getting into Fetterman. Several complaints were made against him by the Officers, but I took no notice of them. If I am to play the Brig Gen, I must trust my Battalion Comdrs in such things. I will however take an opportunity to let him know I dont approve of such speed.

We are now only 10 miles from Ft Fetterman & all hands are looking forward to it, as the first glimpse of civilization. I would have camped further up the creek, but that there was no

182. General Crook arrived at Fort Fetterman on December 28 and left for Fort Laramie three days later, en route to Cheyenne, Wyoming Territory. See Dodge's entry for January 6, 1877.

water to be found This camp is almost waterless, a little alkaline & discolored fluid having been discovered under 15 inches of ice – in the holes that we found passable water in when we passed here before –[183] The country is miserable, almost a true desert – much broken & cut up. No wood, no water – scarce any grass. Nothing to relieve the eye, but a scanty growth of sage brush & all covered with a mantle of white – While I & my staff were lying around a sage brush fire on the snow after our arrival, & while waiting for the wagons, a young Lieut began descanting on pic-nics, their pleasures & discomforts. I spoke up very seriously, "Why should there be anything in the color, Green, <which> to give it a preference over other colors? You eulogize green grass, green leaves & all things green. Is not the mantle, that Mother Earth now wears as becoming to the eye – as soft to the touch. Why should

only

pic-nics be identified ^ with verdancy?" The stare of surprise of the youngster & the grin of appreciation of the oldsters, was sufficient reward for my effort at moralizing. We brought wood – camp bad, no wood water nor grass. Distance 20 miles —

December 29, 1876. Fort Fetterman

Reveille at 6:30. Broke camp 7.30. The night was very cold, so cold that I could not sleep & sometime before morning I got up & made a fire after which, I had a very delightful nap. The sunrise was extraordinarily gorgeous – something I have never seen before Very near the horizon <to>in the east, was a horizontal streak of light so brilliant as to be trying to the eyes – just above one less brilliant <&c> – & another & another each less brilliant than the other until the colors melted

183. Bourke described the water at Sage Creek as "black & greenish like writing ink, and putrid with Sulphuratted Hydrogen" (diary, December 28, 1876, Bourke Papers).

at last into the cold gray of the zenith. From the sun which could not yet be seen, came up what appeared a vast spout of flame, passing through all the colors & reaching to beyond 45°. To the right of the sun, & some 20° away was a brilliant portion of a rain bow. The gradation in color of the horizontal streaks of cloud & color gave an idea of immeasurable distance. It seemed as if one were looking at a landscape of thousands of miles in extent, from the very center of which arose the vast funnel or spout of flame. I have seen the Sun Dog but a few times in my life – but the one this morning was well worth early rising to see. The day was very cold – not so cold as our Xmas – but second only to it. The ther[momete]r was at this post, 2<7>8° below zero this morning at reveille, & with us it got no lower for several hours.

I reached this post about 11 a.m, went up to see Genl Crook whom I joined at Col Carlton's Qrs –[184] paid him or rather them quite a long visit. I am to take the Arty & 23d Infy to the R. R. via Fort Laramie We start on the day after tomorw – I have authority to order Officers & Sergts of 23d to go in advance of the Comd to Omaha Bks & get all the property ready for transportation Went to Sutlers store & saw everybody. Stayed until my wagons got in, & though I was very careful to drink only a spoonful at a time, I found myself nearly tight when I came out into the cold air.

There is nothing new beyond what we have had in our mails No letters or anything for us here. It has moderated very much, & with a good fire of pine wood in my tent, I am more comfortable than I have been in a week. Among the minor discomforts of which I spoke a few days ago, I should have mentioned poor wood. With a stove crammed full of the dryest Cotton wood the tent is not heated. One can keep warm by sitting over the stove – but there is little real comfort

184. Major Caleb H. Carlton, Third Cavalry, whom Dodge designates by his brevet rank, had assumed command at Fort Fetterman on November 15.

General Crook's headquarters, Fort Fetterman (*Harper's Weekly*, December 16, 1876)

in the tent – Another great discomfort is the lack of water for washing – not only our faces & hands but our clothing has to go without, and I have on now a suit of underclothing which I have had on for three weeks.

I froze my nose slightly today, but dont think it will hurt me anyway – My Ku Klux nose & mouth piece strikes across my nose leaving a slit for the eyes. My frozen part was just where the top of this piece touched my nose. My breath froze on the cloth & that froze the bridge of my nose. Met Mrs Carlton today She is a sister of Pollock 9th Infy, & daughter of the old bookseller of Harrisburg.[185] I used to know her when she was a girl, before her marriage. She is not pretty – never was, pettite, & wears huge eyeglasses. She was rather frigid, which I dont yet know if mere manner, or pique at my not calling on her before I left here – Dr. Hoff invited me to stay at his house, which I declined of course, as I have to march many miles yet & a night sleep in a house would probably give me such a cold as would make me miserable all the rest of my journey — A very quiet evening. Everybody visiting, at the post, or having a Jamboree.

Distance today 10 miles – Good road. Have been marching constantly for 8 days

December 30, 1876. Fort Fetterman

Up late this morning. After breakfast sent the Ad[jutan]t up to Hd Qrs, for orders. Got them by 10 a.m. & all satisfactory. I take my Comd with me to Ft Laramie There I break it up, & leaving 9th & 14th[186] take the Arty & 23d to Cheyenne. I do

185. For much of the period between October 1861 and February 1865, Dodge was stationed in and around Harrisburg, Pennsylvania, serving, among other assignments, as chief mustering and disbursing officer for the U.S. Army in the states of Pennsylvania and Maryland and as superintendent of the volunteer recruiting service in those states (Dodge personnel file, AGO).

186. The companies of the Ninth and Fourteenth Infantry, under Major Edwin F. Townsend, were to remain at Fort Laramie awaiting further orders (PRE Order Book, p. 102, Bourke Papers).

not take it for I am authorized to go on to Cheyenne by stage & direct to Omaha – so as to have my things packed by the time the troops reach there

Several other officers go with me. After getting through all my work I went up to the Post to call on the Ladies – Visited Mrs Carlton Mrs Andrews, Bubb, Hoff & Ferris.[187] Dined with Andrews & had another invitation to Carlton's, but too late. Had already accepted, & have not the capacity to emulate Pollock. He yesterday recd two invitations one to dine at 3, another to dine at 5. He accepted both, & ate both dinners.[188] I told the story on him today Paid Rockwell's Com[missar]y bill – also paid the Post Trader – Clarke[189] Paid the Post Comy bill – Came back to camp about 5. p.m. & remained there, though invited to whist & cribbage parties It is a very hospitable post, & the officers all live well. It has been wretched weather, not cold but snowed nearly all day. It is clear & lovely tonight but colder. Orders issued for early start tomorw. Mackenzie left today[190]

December 31, 1876. La Bonté Creek

Wagons reported late & too few of them – so the main portion of my Comd did not get fairly started until 9 am, while

187. The wives, respectively, of Major Carlton, the post commander; Captain William H. Andrews, Third Cavalry; First Lieutenant John W. Bubb, Fourth Infantry; Assistant Surgeon John V.R. Hoff, the post surgeon; and Captain Samuel T. Ferris, Fourth Infantry.

188. This was Captain Otis W. Pollock of Dodge's regiment, not Captain Edwin Pollock, Ninth Infantry, who was still on duty at Cantonment Reno. Otis Pollock was a favorite of Dodge's. A detailed summary of his career to 1883 is in L. R. Hamersley, *Records of Living Officers of the United States Army*, pp. 340–41.

189. This person was likely an employee of the authorized post trader, E. Tillotson, who lived in Sioux City, Iowa, and was often absent from the post.

190. Colonel Mackenzie was on his way east, first to Chicago, to report to General Sheridan, and then to Washington, D.C. President Grant wished him to command all troops in the nation's capital in the event of a national emergency arising from the still disputed presidential election. See Nohl, "Bad Hand," pp. 228–29; Pierce, *The Most Promising Young Officer*, p. 194; Robinson, *Bad Hand*, p. 232.

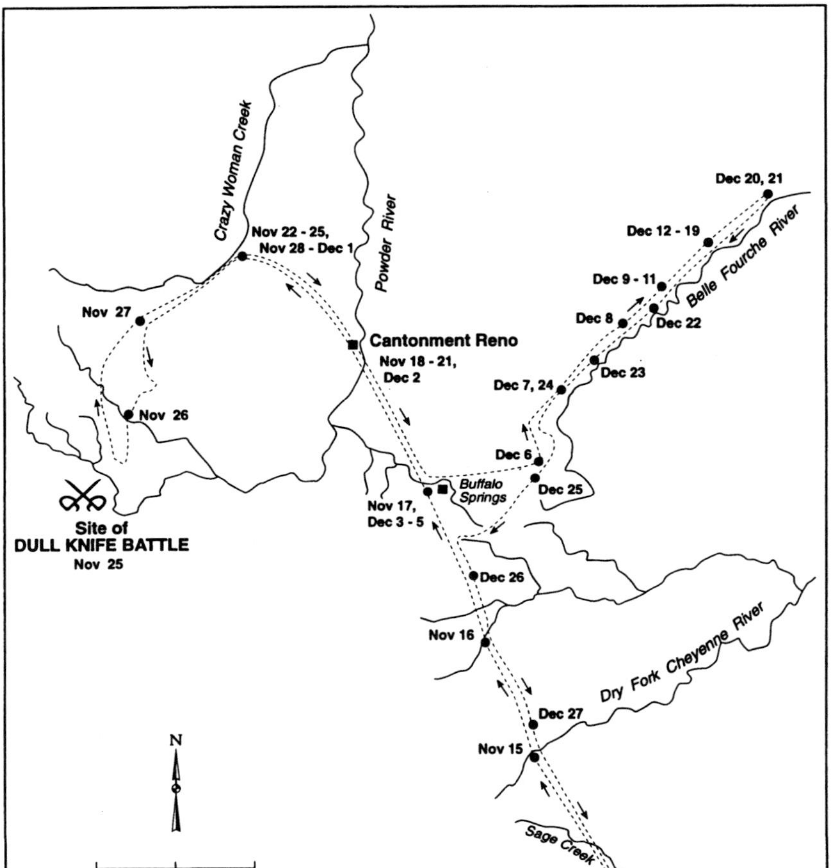

Dodge's itinerary, November 13–December 30, 1876

the Comps of 23d Infy which were short of wagons, did not get off until about 10 am Road abominable – up & down the steepest kind of hills all the time. It is difficult to conceive of a more broken country. The Laramie range of Mountains is just on our right, the Platte river on our left. The waters in their headlong course of only a few miles have cut deep gorges & left high & broken back bones across which the road twists & turns in innumerable windings. Besides this the winds have brought vast quantities of snow from the high places & deposited it in the valleys & ravines. Many times today our wagons were to the hubs in snow & our camp tonight in the valley of La Bonté Ck is covered to the depth of at least 12 inches on a level, & in many places the drifts are from 3 to 5 feet deep. It has however been a very good day. The wind was sharp but in our backs, & towards the afternoon that died out. Tonight is lovely not cold nor windy & a lovely moon – but indications at a distance of more snow before morning. We will be lucky if we get through without a blockade. Genl Crook started this morning for Cheyenne – by the cut-off, & expects to be there in five days – The marching was very hard today but my men are so tough now that I can guarantee any amt of hard marching. It is only the mules I am afraid of.[191] We have however plenty of forage & I hope will get through without trouble or delay. If possible I shall make Ft Laramie on the 3d Jany, – for I wish to take the stage on the a.m. of the 4th for Cheyenne. Dined with Clark & Rockwell. Had a splendid dinner for Camp – Roast Turkey & other nice things – Did ample justice to it all. Good camp – wood water & grass. Distance 20 ms

The last day of the Centennial year. In view of all the election rows, of the hardships of a winter Campaign, & of my verging on to my 50th year,[192] I could moralize quite lively tonight but that I am sleepy & have given orders for a very early

191. Dodge wrote "off."
192. Dodge's birthdate was May 19, 1827.

start tomorw. Morality is a good thing in Civilization, but worth nothing, means nothing, here

January 1, 1877. Horseshoe Creek

Reveille at 5.30, broke camp at 6.40 a most excellent start for the New Year. The road is a terrible one – rising one or two thousand feet above the valley of La Bonté on to an immense ridge all that remains of what was once the great plain stretching away to the N. & East from the foot of the Laramie Range of Mts. Up & down all day. In many places the drifted snow was up to the knees of the men & mules, and in some few places still deeper. The men marched admirably – under the most trying circumstances, & got to our camping place on Horseshoe Creek at 2.40 pm. – making all things considered, almost unprecedented march. <W>The wagons got along well also & all were in by 3.30 pm. To my great surprise I found encamped here Mackenzie's whole Command He started from Fetterman a day before me, & I have made in two days a distance that he made in three – so much for Infantry after it is well seasoned. Mackenzie himself has gone to Chicago & his Cavy is under Comd of Capt Mauck.[193]

I have had a hard day. I never felt better than when I got up this am but when lighting my pipe after breakfast a puff of wind blew some sparks into my face – one into my eye, which raised a small blister on the eyeball. It has given me great pain all day, & I could hardly see. It is better tonight & I hope will be all right in the morning.

About 10 Ock I was taken with griping pains in my bowels, & have had a severe dysentery all day, & between that & the burned eye, I have cause to remember my 1st Jany 77. That is better tonight but I am rather weak.

193. Captain Clarence V. Mauck, Fourth Cavalry, had commanded a battalion under Colonel Mackenzie.

Have a nice Camp, wood water & grass as good as can be found out here. I signed up all the records of my Comd at night. Made out the Mess bill. Wrote the orders relieving Officers from duty to go in ahead of the Comd from Fort Laramie. Wrote also rough draft of Genl Order breaking up the Command.

The day has been quite mild. It is a real treat to go for a whole day without our breath freezing to our beards in icicles – but this is the first day of such a marvel for several weeks. We must be getting south. It thawed considerably, & when not in damp snow the men marched in mud. Tonight is stormy – wind and occasional snow. Distance 20 miles – (called anywhere from 18 to 22 –)

January 2, 1877. Warm Springs

Reveille 5.30, broke camp 6.30. Every wagon & the rear guard were out of camp & well started on the road by 7 a.m. & while the morning star was still bright in the east. Last night the weather was very threatening, & it was a good chance that today would be abominable. It cleared off lovely however, & the day has been all that could be desired except that it was rather too warm for us in our winter trappings. Though the country is even more broken, & much more picturesque than that passed yesterday & the day before the road is much better & we all came along – men & wagons – without difficulty We were told in advance that it was a long march, not less than 26 miles – & I was very agreeably disappointed to reach the camping ground at 2 pm The troops arrived at 3.15 & the wagons were all in by 4.30.

It is a very pretty camp in a narrow valley enclosed in pine & cedar covered bluffs of 3 or 400 feet high From the base of one of these a large spring bursts out, & forms a brook which runs away to the river. The water of this spring is warm not hot, – but more than tepid – too warm to be palateable for drinking until it has been allowed to cool.

No sooner had they arrived in camp than Townsend & Egan posted away to Fort Laramie. I should have gone too, had a wife been waiting for me, as for them.

It has been a long march but all things considered one of the pleasantest of our long trip. Weather & scenery have combined to make it enjoyable. Got up my last orders to be published tomorw. Saw Fury in reference to trains to go down with Arty & 23d. Fixed all satisfactorily & went to bed. Distance 23 miles

January 3, 1877. Fort Laramie, W.T.

Reveille at 6.30. Broke camp at 7.30 everything being ahead of us. Had a pleasant march over a fairly good road for 13 miles to this post, where I arrived at 11 am, the command getting in an hour later. Called on the Comdg Off, Major Evans 3d Cavy at once.[194] Then went down & put the Comd in Camp & returned to Evans for lunch, to which I did most ample justice. After this I made arrangements for an ambulance tomorw to take me to Cheyenne & came back to my tent to pack up. Got out all my citizen clothing – one rather dilapidated suit – packed my trunk & valise – gave Clark a list of the things he is to take care of for me.[195] Issued all my orders breaking up the Comd[196] & ordering some officers to Courts &c –[197] getting

194. Major Andrew W. Evans, Third Cavalry, had relieved Major Edwin F. Townsend as post commander at Fort Laramie upon Townsend's departure for service in the Powder River Expedition.

195. The quartermaster of Dodge's command, First Lieutenant William L. Clarke, Twenty-third Infantry, was to march to Cheyenne with Company G.

196. In G.O. 13, dated January 3, 1877, at Fort Laramie, Dodge commended the discipline and spirit of his men "under very trying circumstances." He expressed regret that "the fortunes of war gave them no opportunity of showing as good conduct in battle as they have displayed endurance and fortitude in all the hardships privations and suffering incident to a winter campaign in this terrible country" (Order Book, HQIAB).

197. Captain Joseph B. Campbell, Fourth Artillery; Captain David Krause, Fourteenth Infantry; and Second Lieutenant John A. Baldwin, Ninth Infantry, were to report to North Platte Station, Nebraska, as witnesses in a general court-martial of Captain Edward H. Leib, Fifth Cavalry (S.O. 26, Order Book, HQIAB).

through in time to go back to Evans' to dinner at dark Remained with him an hour after dinner when Randall & I went to the Billiard room. Played 2 games with Pollock coming out even – bade good by to such officers as were present & went down again to Camp. I take Randall Pollock & Dodge with me in ambulance tomorw, the other detached officers go on stage next day. Campbell is grouty & put out because I do not take him in ambulance with me but I take care of my own first.[198] Besides all will get to Cheyenne in time to take the same train that I expect to get.

Telegram from Crook late at night, directing the train, and consequently the troops to remain here for one day, to rest the mules. The mules are doubtless satisfied but the humans are disgusted

Cold nasty wind today but it always blows here. Tonight is not so bad. Last night in camp of this most disagreeable winter campaign. Thank Heaven!!

Distance today 13 miles

January 4, 1877. Philips Ranche, Chugwater

Ambulance reported late, with a very poor team of broken down Cavalry horses – However we got off before 8 a.m. – The road was very bad, snow in drifts sometimes nearly to the *Hubs* – and the side hills slippery with ice. Arrived at Owen's Ranche (Chugwater Springs)[199] about 1 pm and had dinner. After getting into the valley of the Chug the road was good & we bolled along splendidly, considering our team, & arrived at Philips just after dark. Had a good supper & excellent room and bed. It has been very cold & blustery today but we were covered with buffalo robes & quite comfortable.

Distance 45 miles.

198. By "my own" Dodge means officers of his own regiment.

199. The Owen ranch was approximately twenty-five miles south of Fort Laramie; the ranch of "Portugee" Philips, where Dodge had spent a night on May 9, 1875, was twenty miles farther.

January 5, 1877. Lodge Pole Creek

Up early & got a good start, hoping to make Cheyenne today, but the snow was so deep & the road so slippery & bad, going up & down the numberless hills, & our team so poor, that we only arrived at Horse Creek about 2 p.m. where we nooned & lunched. Then went on to Pole Creek, arriving just before dark. Good supper, but rather poor sleeping accommodations Distance 22 miles.

January 6, 1877. Cheyenne

Up early & got a good start The road proving much better than we expected, we got along well, & by 11.30 am safely landed at the R.R. Hotel Cheyenne. The Reynolds Court Martial is in session – commenced today – & the town is full of officers.[200] More Rank than I have seen together since the war. Pope, Crook, King, Gibbon, Sykes, Flint & lots of others too numerous to mention.[201] Pope told me to take my time about getting to my new post, which is to be Fort Riley,[202] so I determined to stay over here a day & see all the folks. Pollock

200. The court-martial of Colonel Joseph J. Reynolds, Third Cavalry, and Captain Alexander Moore of the same regiment was convened at Cheyenne on January 5 and continued through January 19, 1877. At the time Dodge was in the city more than one hundred army officers were also present as members of the court, witnesses, or in other capacities. The charges against the two officers had been filed by General Crook and pertained to their behavior in an engagement with Sioux Indians under Crazy Horse the previous March 17.

201. Brigadier General John Pope presided at the Reynolds-Moore court-martial. Except for General Crook, who was a witness, the other persons mentioned by Dodge were also members of the court. They included Colonel John H. King, Ninth Infantry; Colonel John Gibbon, Seventh Infantry; Colonel George Sykes, Twentieth Infantry; and Colonel Franklin F. Flint, Fourth Infantry. A photograph showing the members of the general court-martial is in Hedren, *Fort Laramie in 1876*, p. 217.

202. In earlier years Fort Riley had been important to the U.S. Army for its proximity to the confluence of the Republican and Smoky Hill Rivers. Although at this period the strategic significance of the post had decreased, its location near the junction of several railroads gave it continuing military value. Fort Riley was garrisoned by only two companies.

& Dodge took the cars, as they have to stop at Sidney.[203] Had a delightful evening mostly spent in Pope's room where there was quite a crowd. Mrs Crook is here looking fat & jolly as ever,[204] & the Genl himself was more cordial than he ever was to me before. Jeff Davis <was> is on the Court, & he & Crook spent the evening in Pope's room – both very quiet – Randall & I had same room at Hotel – but he did [not] bother me –
Distance 18 miles.

January 7, 1877. On cars

No Court today it being Sunday, so I spent the morning "gassing" with the old fellows. I find myself quite a hero & an authority, (though I knew as much before I went on this Expedition as I do on my return) except in the matter of managing Indians, & Crook is the best teacher in that branch of knowledge I ever saw. Took the cars at 2.30 p.m. Got a stateroom for our quartette for Randal goes down with me, & Pollock and Dodge are to join tonight at Sidney.

January 8, 1877. Omaha Barracks

<At L> Arrived at Omaha late, our train having last night run into a herd of Cattle sleeping on the track – mashing them up, & throwing engine & some cars off the track. I slept through it all, half-waking occasionally & wondering what the train stopped so often for. I remember concluding that I must wake on the stopping of the cars at the different stations – like the miller who wakes when his mill stops – I was surprised next

203. Both officers needed to gather their personal effects at Sidney Barracks before proceeding to Fort Leavenworth.

204. Mrs. Crook was the former Mary Tapscott Dailey of Moorefield, Virginia. She resided at the general's family estate near Oakland, Maryland. The couple had no children and saw each other only sporadically. During her husband's lengthy absences on duty, between 1871 and 1878, Mrs. Crook compiled a detailed scrapbook recording his exploits as they were recounted in major newspapers (Crook Papers). Unlike the general, Mrs. Crook was gregarious and enjoyed attending social functions.

a.m. to find we had been delayed for 7 hours in one spot. An ambulance was waiting for us at Depot, & getting in we started for the post. Just outside the fence of the Garrison is a bridge over a small ravine. It was very cold & we were all shut up in the ambulance & just as we arrived at this bridge there was a twist & a jolt, then a dead halt. I opened the door & jumped out to find all the mules gone. The leaders had swerved at the bridge, run the front of the ambulance diagonally against one of the posts of the railing, then came straight with a plunge, broke the tongue sharp off at the hounds & all went for the stable. It was a narrow escape for us, for if the tongue had not broken the post would, & we would have been tumbled into the ravine. So the greatest danger I encountered on my great winter expedition, was at my own post, & at the very last moment of the Expedition.

We walked to our houses. I woke up Joe & Laura had a bed prepared for Randall, & we were soon in the land of Nod – Home again safe & sound, & as I drew the clean sheets about me, I could not resist a sigh of relief & thankfulness.

And thus after 67 days of hardship & exposure I am again at home all right & comfortable.[205]

205. Pages [71]–[74] and [75R], which follow in the notebook, are blank. On p. [75V] Dodge wrote a list of "Camps & distances, on Return trip from Camp." Here he recorded the distances from "5 Belle Fourche" to Fort Fetterman, calculating in a separate column the aggregate miles marched beginning at Medicine Bow. On the inside back cover he completed the listing, recording distances traveled from Fort Fetterman to Cheyenne. According to his tabulation, the itinerary of his command from Medicine Bow to Cheyenne totaled 633 miles.

Journal Four: Winter 1876–1877

Powder River
Campaign
Winter
1876–7
No 4[206]

Resumé

A winter campaign is a terrible ordeal for Troops, but it is really the most effective against Indians, who cannot stand cold as well as whites, nor can they travel rapidly with their half famished skeletons of horses. Take it in its entirety our Campaign has been a marked success The Cheyennes have received a blow such as they have never had before, & from which they will not soon recover. While the hostile Sioux under Crazy Horse have[207] been compelled to move their village not less than twice – to leave the game region of the Rosebud in which they had pitched their winter camp, and to take refuge in the

206. This manuscript journal consists of seventy-five unnumbered pages in a copy of "Pocket Scratch Book No. 4," a stiff cardboard pad measuring 3 3/8 x 4 7/8 inches, to which are attached sheets of plain unlined paper. Although the pad is designed to permit easy ripping away of its individual slips, in this case all the original pages are present. On the bottom side of the cardboard pad Dodge wrote in black ink, "Winter Campaign [/] 1876." Except as noted here, the journal is written entirely in pencil. Pages [1V] and [26V]–[75V] are blank. The text begins on p. [2R].

207. Dodge wrote "has."

barren inhospitable and comparatively gameless bad lands of the Little Missouri They have learned by sad experience that at no time & in no place are they safe from the pursuit of the Troops.

Premising this it must yet be conceded that the Campaign has not been so eminently successful as it might have been, and while the facts are fresh in my mind I wish to put on record what in my opinion was the cause of the comparative failure.

Genl Crook has a most wonderful knowledge of the Indian character & this knowledge gives him a power over them which I have never before seen possessed by any one. Nor can I for the life of me understand it, even after seeing him time & again, among the Indians & holding intercourse with them. Among Indians eloquence is a great power. All their instruction must necessarily be oral. Manner also has influence. Genl C. has the worst manner I ever saw,— He has generally very little to say at any "talk" and that little is said in a few words, his eyes downcast, his hands in the pockets of his old gray pants – voice low & hesitating – & in all respects he looks & acts far more like a schoolboy trying to fabricate an excuse for a delinquency than like a general comdg an army.

In spite of all this there is no shadow of a doubt as to the high estimation in which he is held by the Indians. He is a good strategist, ^has wonderful tenacity of purpose, will & pluck, & is entirely careless of personal discomfort He lacks but one thing to be a very great man – that is, *Administrative ability*.

He can decide how many & what troops to take into the field with him, but there his power ends. How to fit them out, & care for them afterwards is a problem, which to him has no solution. His ignorance of such things is remarkable & painful. It is even ludicrous, for he carries it to such an extent, as to regard with the most profound admiration any man who evinces even a moderate ability in this direction. He must be fully aware of his own deficiency in this respect, for having selected Officers to do this work for him, he never interferes in any way, by order or suggestion, & when he gets hold of a man who does tolerably well, he can never admire him sufficiently or praise him enough. This would be admirable did he only get hold of first class men, but though a fair judge of human nature, he yet in the nature of things sometimes gets a man unequal to his work. The success of an expedition depends more on the administrative ability of the Staff, than the genius of the General – & this is more true in Indian, than in Civilized Warfare – for in the former, each army, or active force must depend entirely on itself for everything. On the purely Military Organization of our Winter Expedition I have no comments to make, except that at its start General C. had not yet succeeded in divesting himself of a certain contempt for – or rather an undervaluing of the Infantry Arm.

When he was about starting on the Rosebud Campaign,[208] I said "Genl I wish you would take me & 6 or 8 Cos of the Regt with you." "Why what" replied he "could I do with Infantry against Indians?["] "Everything["] I said "that you can do with cavalry, except perhaps dash in & capture stock – but that inability will be more than compensated by the better & steadier fighting they will do." "Well" he answered "I dont think Infantry any account against Indians, though I do expect to take a Couple of Comps as escort for the wagon train" –

"Well Genl" I said "you of course will do as you please, but the very best campaigns ever made against Indians in this country, were made by Infantry. Let me have the management of the men for the first three weeks, & after that I will guaranté to march just as far & as long as the Cavy & to run down the Indian stock, provided only that you keep me supplied with rations" —

It was of no use. He couldn't be talked into any opinion of the staying qualities of Infantry against Indians —

208. General Crook's second expedition of 1876 against the Sioux and Cheyennes left Fort Fetterman on May 29.

Long after this, & after the battle of the Rosebud I asked him – rather to his surprise "if" he did not think of me during that battle? He laughed at the recollection, & said, "Well Dodge, when my Cavalry got scattered all over creation, & I
it
could not get ^ together, or to obey orders, I did wish for a few companies of the Old Regt.["][209] However even yet he was not cured of his prejudice, for he thinks to this day that the Battle of Rosebud was lost through the neglect & indispo-
of some
sition ^ of the Cavy Officers to do their duty, while I, though not there know that it was lost for lack of Infantry.[210]

However Mackenzies affair cured him of all that Cavalry foolishness & he will never again go out with a preponderating Cavalry force.[211] His ideas in regard to the use of a large force

209. That is, the Twenty-third Infantry, Crook's former unit.

210. The Battle of the Rosebud, on June 17, 1876, was waged along a line of engagement that at one point extended over almost five miles. The battle was fought in broken terrain where cavalry units could not maneuver effectively and had difficulty communicating. A suggestive photograph of the battle site is in Hedren, *Traveler's Guide to the Great Sioux War*, p. 52. Dodge believed that the presence of infantry would have helped integrate the U.S. forces and would have added to the kinds of military operations they could perform.

211. Dodge's confident assertion was not borne out by Crook's subsequent operations against the escaped Northern Cheyennes in Nebraska, the Utes of Colorado, and the Apaches of Arizona Territory. Logistical support by a well-conditioned packtrain and intelligence gathered by large numbers of native scouts remained key features of Crook's later field service, whatever he may have decided about the relative value of infantry versus cavalry in campaigns against Indians.

Colonel Mackenzie seems to have shared some of the views of both Crook and Dodge. As he prepared for a campaign against the Utes in the fall of 1879, he besieged his superiors with demands for additional wagon and pack mule transportation, sought to obtain Captain George M. Randall with as many as 100 Cheyenne scouts for service with his command, and asked for a complement of approximately 700 infantry and only 200 cavalry. In mountainous terrain in severe winter conditions, he observed to General Sheridan on October 30, 1879, "I believe a large Cavalry command will not be so efficient as the same number of Infantry." General Pope, commander of the Department of the Missouri, noted in his endorsement of this message:

of friendly Indians were admirable & carried out with great ability – His management of the troops was sufficiently good, except where an improvement would have brought him in collision with one of his Staff. But having said this, I have given him all the credit I can & I now have to speak of his deficiencies —

All the supplies for his expedition had to be collected & forwarded by the Chiefs of Staff who were in Omaha.[212] With these Officers he never once communicated for nearly eight months. They knew nothing of the force he intended to take with him[,] of the time he expected to be out, nor even of the point which was to be his base of supplies. His own field staff issued orders to Companies in various parts of the Dept to join him, & it was only from these orders that the Chiefs of Staff were enabled to guess how many troops he had, & where he would start from – As it was they were forced, in order to be surely right, to accumulate very large supplies at three different places – Fetterman, Laramie, & Red Cloud – & for lack of timely information the supply of forage at Fort Fetterman was never sufficient –

When I left to join Crook Bob Williams implored me to write to him by every mail, & give him all the information I could pick up, as to how many men & animals, how long we would be out, & where we expected to go. "For" said he, "we are now working entirely in the dark & by guess, & any item you may give us, may be of great service to us & to you" ——

"Whilst I agree with [Mackenzie] about the superiority of infantry for such service in the Mountains during the winter, I have, as you know, no more Infantry than I have already sent him, which can possibly be sent" (Ute Campaign Special File). At the time of this correspondence, Colonel Dodge was in command at Cantonment North Fork Canadian River, Indian Territory. The following spring he received orders to join Mackenzie at Fort Garland, Colorado, and to command the infantry companies in Mackenzie's operations in the mountains of Colorado that summer.

212. Dodge refers to Major Marshall I. Ludington, chief quartermaster for the Department of the Platte; Major John P. Hawkins, chief commissary of subsistence; and Lieutenant Colonel Robert Williams, adjutant general.

The field staff of the expedition was excellent with the single exception of the Quarter Master. This was Capt Fury, a regular Q. M. an industrious energetic hard-working man – a gentleman in manners & education, & with the disposition to be a good officer. He did the very best he could, but he did not know *how* to do. Consequently we all suffered & the Campaign was a failure. Fury had a train of over 250 wagons, & 300 pack mules. The fighting force of the Comd was about 1650 men. The non combattants swelled the number of mouths to feed to about 2000. With the means of transpn at our disposal we should have taken[213] 40 days rations for the whole Comd & 1/2 forage for 30 days, & yet had ample wagons for all the extra Qr Mr. things, iron horse shoes &c &c, that were necessary –

Instead of this we never had at any time more than 15 days rations, & 1/2 forage for the same time. Consequently we were never in condition to pull away from our base for more than a week at a time. When we left Fetterman we had 62 days rations with us or at that base, but our supply of forage was short all the time – Most of the rations left at Fetterman were sent to Reno for us so that at all times we had an ample supply at the latter place.

Now we will see where the trouble was with the wagon train, that it could only haul less than half its capacity.

Before we left Fort Fetterman the troops had been reduced to 3 blankets per man – a common tent to every 4, & a sibbley stove to every 8 men.[214] When the wagons were sent to the Cos to be loaded up, it was found that each teamster had a roll of bedding larger than any Officer of the Comd – while every 3d or 4th wagon<s> was half full of utensils of all sorts – It

213. This long statement evolves in a direction that makes "could have taken" the better verb.

214. These allowances conform to the limits specified in Dodge's own G.O. 3, November 11, 1876, HQIAB. See also the Bourke diary for November 11, 1876, Bourke Papers.

soon transpired that each 2 wagon Masters (& there were about a dozen) had a wall tent, Sibley stove & bedding ad lib. Each 4 teamsters had a wall tent & Sibley stove. Each eight teamsters had an extra wall tent a huge 4 or 6 plate cooking stove (none of the troops were allowed them) a large mess chest, with plates &c, as many boxes, barrels &c of supplies as they chose to carry – & an extra man to cook for them – who of course had his extra allowance of baggage The consequence was that the 300 teamsters wagon masters & cooks had more actual weight & bulk of baggage than all the Officers and men of the whole fighting force, 1650 men, put together.

Nor was this all. The teamsters were under no sort of discipline & did just as they pleased. Getting into Camp late they would unhitch the mules, tie them to the tongue, throw a little corn into the food box & then disappear, to be seen no more by any of the troops, until such time as it suited them to put in an appearance in the morning. All went off to the general train to sleep & eat. It seems almost incredible, yet I state it as a fact, that on many occasions my rear guard had to remain in camp until half-past 9 or 10 Ock am, waiting for the teamsters to hitch the mules to the wagons, which had been loaded & ready to move since half past 6 a.m. This condition of affairs was intolerable & I quarrelled with Fury & with Genl Crook about it until I felt like a common scold & was ashamed of myself. But not infrequently my men would get into Camp by 2 or 3 pm, & have to wait in the snow until long after dark without shelter or food – & all because the teamsters were too lazy to get up in the morning – It was a most infernal outrage, & would not have been tolerated an instant, by any Comdg Officer that I know of except Genl Crook.

On Christmas Day the mercury was frozen in the bulb. My Comd got off in good season 6.30. Some of the wagons not being hitched up I waited until 9.30 am, then left in disgust. I arrived in camp after a march of over twenty miles – & joined Genl C. & staff around a camp fire. I was very angry & went after the Genl. strong – I told him it was an outrage on my men – on human nature, & demanded that some steps be taken to remedy the evil. He looked at me in a helpless sort of way for a moment then walked away without a word. I then went for the Staff, all of whom held their peace. At last Fury's chief clerk standing near said, "It cant be helped Colonel, the teamsters have a ring & if we were to discharge one, a hundred would go" "Well let them go" I said "I will give you a better man in the place of every scoundrel who leaves. Put them off in the prarie here & let them go" – The clerk subsided, & Mackenzie who was by hooked his arm into mine <&> led me over to his tent, & gave me a drink.

"I think" said he "you are too hard on Fury. He does the best he can" – "Admitted" I replied, "but that best leads to suffering of my men, & it is time somebody was put in his place, who can do better than Fury's best." "You have your own Qr Mr & your train is under your own control. The Genl will not allow me to have Control of mine. My men suffer yours dont, & there is all the difference" –[215]

The very next night I happened to walk over to Head Qrs, & found Mackenzie giving it to poor Fury worse than I had ever done – so hard was he indeed, that he afterwards apologized to me, & said he was sorry he had said so many mean things to Fury —

Another result of this condition of affairs was that the teamsters took no sort of care of their mules. In the whole trip, though out & among the wagons at all hours, I never saw a mule curried or a wagon greased. Once or twice orders were given to herd the mules at night. The order was obeyed by turning the mules loose & driving them off some distance from Camp Then all the teamsters (who should have remained with the

215. Dodge's response to Mackenzie begins with "Admitted" and ends at this point. He included needless quotation marks between the first and second sentences.

mules) came back & went to bed. The consequence was that next morning the mules were scattered for miles, & took hours to find & collect together. This was done only a very few times, & the poor mules as a rule had nothing whatever to eat, except a pint or two of corn. Of course they were soon starved out, & broken down. Had the mules been properly taken care of, we ought to have lost none – for our marches were short & by no means continuous. In the whole two months we marched but little over 400 miles.[216] There were however very many mules broken down & abandoned, & this result was not due to hard work, but simply & purely to neglect. Had Trout been Quarter Master of that Comd we would not have lost a half dozen mules all told –

The lack of knowledge & management in the Qr Mr entailed unnecessary suffering on the men, lost many mules to the Govt & caused the failure of the expedition – for had we been supplied with <suff>as much rations & forage as we could have carried, we could have marched three times as far, & probably struck Crazy Horse

216. By Dodge's calculation, during the forty-seven days of its absence from Fort Fetterman, between November 13 and December 29, the command marched 401 miles.

Bibliography

MANUSCRIPT MATERIALS

Blackmore, William. Papers. Manuscript Division, Museum of New Mexico, Santa Fe.

Bourke, John Gregory. Papers. Special Collections Division, U.S. Military Academy, West Point, N.Y.

Crook, George. Papers. U.S. Army Military History Institute, Carlisle Barracks, Pa.

Crook-Kennan Papers. U.S. Army Military History Institute, Carlisle Barracks, Pa.

Dodge, Richard Irving. Papers, 1865–1949. Everett D. Graff Collection of Western Americana, Newberry Library, Chicago.

Indian Wars Miscellaneous Collection. U.S. Army Military History Institute, Carlisle Barracks, Pa.

Miles, Nelson A. Papers. U.S. Army Military History Institute, Carlisle Barracks, Pa.

Order of the Indian Wars Collection. U.S. Army Military History Institute, Carlisle Barracks, Pa.

Secretary of War. Letters Sent Relating to Military Affairs, 1876. National Archives and Records Administration. Record Group 107. Microcopy M6, Rolls 72, 73.

U.S. Army. Adjutant General's Office. Richard Irving Dodge Personnel File. National Archives and Records Administration. Record Group 94.

———. Department of the Platte. Field Records. Powder River Expedition. Letters Sent, November–December 1876; Endorsements Sent; Letters Received, General and Special Orders Issued, Charges and Specifications, and Returns. National Archives and Records Administration. Record Group 393.

———. Division of the Missouri. Field Records. Fort Garland Column, 1880. National Archives and Records Administration. Record Group 393.

———. Division of the Missouri. Sioux War Special File, 1876–77. National Archives and Records Administration. Record Group 393. Microcopy No. 1495, Reel 4.

———. Division of the Missouri. Ute Campaign Special File, 1879–80. National Archives and Records Administration. Record Group 393. Microcopy No. 1495, Reel 7.

———. Field Records. Powder River Expedition. Headquarters, Infantry and Artillery Battalions. Order Book; Endorsement and Letter Book. National Archives and Records Administration. Record Group 393.

———. Fort Fetterman Post Returns, 1867–82. National Archives and Records Administration. Record Group 94. Microcopy No. 617, Reel 365.

———. Fort Laramie Post Returns, 1861–76. National Archives and Records Administration. Record Group 94. Microcopy No. 617, Reel 596.

———. Fort Riley Post Returns, 1872–84. National Archives and Records Administration. Record Group 94. Microcopy No. 617, Reel 1013.

———. Fourteenth Infantry Regimental Returns, 1873–82. National Archives and Records Administration. Record Group 94. Microcopy No. M665, Reel 155.

———. Fourth Cavalry Regimental Returns, 1877–83. National Archives and Records Administration. Record Group 94. Microcopy No. M744, Reel 43.

———. Ninth Infantry Regimental Returns, 1870–79. National Archives and Records Administration. Record Group 94. Microcopy No. M665, Reel 104.

———. Omaha Barracks Post Returns, 1874–85. National Archives and Records Administration. Record Group 94. Microcopy No. 617, Reel 880.

———. Second Cavalry Regimental Returns, 1872–79. National Archives and Records Administration. Record Group 94. Microcopy No. M744, Reel 19.

———. Third Cavalry Regimental Returns, 1876–84. National Archives and Records Administration. Record Group 94. Microcopy No. M744, Reel 31.

———. Twenty-third Infantry Regimental Returns, 1874–82. National Archives and Records Administration. Record Group 94. Microcopy No. M665, Reel 237.

GOVERNMENT PUBLICATIONS

Official Army Register. Washington, D.C.: Government Printing Office, 1874–82.

U.S. Congress. House. *Report of the Commissioner of Indian Affairs* (1876). Executive Documents No. 1, Part 5, 44th Congress, 2nd Session. Serial 1749.

———. House. *Report of the Commissioner of Indian Affairs* (1877). Executive Documents No. 1, Part 5, 45th Congress, 2nd Session. Serial 1800.

———. House. *Report of the Secretary of War* (1876). Executive Documents No. 1, Part 2, 44th Congress, 2nd Session. Serial 1742.

———. House. *Report of the Secretary of War* (1877). Executive Documents No. 1, Part 2, 45th Congress, 1st Session. Serial 1794.

———. House. *Report of the Secretary of War* (1878). Executive Documents No. 1, Part 2, 45th Congress, 3rd Session. Serial 1843.

———. House. *Report of the Secretary of War* (1880). Executive Documents No. 1, Part, 2, 46th Congress, 2nd Session. Serial 1952.

———. House. *Revised Army Regulations.* Report No. 85, 42nd Congress, 3rd Session (1872). Serial 1576.

U.S. War Department. Adjutant General's Office. General Court-Martial Orders, 1876, 1877.

NEWSPAPERS AND PERIODICALS

Army and Navy Journal, 1876–80, 1895.

Chicago Inter-Ocean, 1876.

Chicago Tribune, 1876.

Harper's Weekly, 1876, 1877.
New York Herald, 1876.
New York Times, 1876.
New York Tribune, 1876.

ARTICLES

Bourke, John G. "Mackenzie's Last Fight with the Cheyennes: A Winter Campaign in Wyoming and Montana." *Journal of the Military Service Institution of the United States* 11 (January 1890): 29–49; (March 1890): 198–221.

Buecker, Thomas, ed. "The Journals of James S. McClellan, 1st Sgt., Company H, 3rd Cavalry." *Annals of Wyoming* 57, no. 1 (spring 1985): 21–34.

Dodge, Richard Irving. "The Enlisted Soldier." *Journal of the Military Service Institution of the United States* 8 (May 1886): 259–318.

Grange, Roger T., Jr. "Fort Robinson: Outpost on the Plains." *Nebraska History* 39, no. 3 (September 1958): 191–240.

Hedren, Paul L., ed. "Campaigning with the 5th Cavalry: Private James B. Frew's Diary and Letters from the Great Sioux War of 1876." *Nebraska History* 65 (winter 1984): 433–66.

Kime, Wayne R. "'Not Coarse . . . But Not Delicate': Richard Irving Dodge's Portrayal of Plains Indians in *The Plains of the Great West and Their Inhabitants*." *Platte Valley Review* 17, no. 1 (winter 1989): 69–83.

King, James T. "Needed: A Re-Evaluation of General George Crook." *Nebraska History* 45 (September 1964): 223–35.

Welty, Raymond L. "Supplying the Frontier Military Posts." *Kansas Historical Quarterly* 7 (May 1938): 154–69.

BOOKS

Aderman, Alice R. *A Genealogy of the Irvings of New York: Washington Irving, His Brothers and Sisters, and Their Dependents*. N.p.: privately published, 1981.

Bourke, John G. *Mackenzie's Last Fight with the Cheyennes: A Winter Campaign in Wyoming and Montana*. Governor's Island, N.Y.: Military Service Institution, 1890.

———. *On the Border with Crook*. New York: Charles Scribner's Sons, 1891.

Brayer, Herbert O. *William Blackmore: A Case Study in the Economic Development of the West*. 2 vols. Denver: Bradford-Robinson, 1949.

Brininstool, E. A. *Crazy Horse: The Invincible Oglalla Sioux Chief.* Los Angeles: Wetzel, 1949.

Brown, Jesse, and A. M. Willard. *The Black Hills Trails*. Rapid City, S.D.: Rapid City Journal Co., 1924.

Butterfield, Consul W. *History of the City of Omaha, Nebraska*. New York: Munsell and Co., 1894.

City Directories of the United States, 1860–1901: Guide to the Microfilm Collection. Woodbridge, Conn.: Research Publications, 1983.

Clark, William P. *The Indian Sign Language: With Brief Explanatory Notes of the Gestures Taught Deaf-Mutes in Our Institutions for Their Instruction, and a Description of Some of the Peculiar Laws, Customs, Myths, Superstitions, Ways of Living, Code of Peace and War Signals of Our Aborigines*. Philadelphia: L. R. Hamersley and Co., 1885.

Collins, John S. *My Experiences in the West*. Edited by Colton Storm. Chicago: Lakeside Press, 1970.

Crook, George. *General George Crook: His Autobiography*. Edited by Martin F. Schmitt. Norman: University of Oklahoma Press, 1960.

Cullum, George W. *Biographical Register of Officers and Graduates of the U.S. Military Academy at West Point, from its Establishment to the Army Re-organization of 1866–67*. 2 vols. New York: D. Van Nostrand, 1868.

———. *Supplement to the Biographical Register.* New York: D. Van Nostrand, 1868.

Danker, Donald F., ed. *Man of the Plains: Recollections of Luther North, 1856–1882*. Introduction by George Bird Grinnell. Lincoln: University of Nebraska Press, 1961.

De Barthe, Joe. *Life and Adventures of Frank Grouard*. Edited by Edgar I. Stewart. Norman: University of Oklahoma Press, 1958.

Dodge, Richard Irving. *The Black Hills: A Minute Description of the Routes, Scenery, Soil, Climate, Timber, Gold, Geology, Zoölogy, etc. With An Accurate Map, Four Sectional Drawings, and Ten Plates from Photographs, Taken on the Spot*. New York: James Miller, 1875.

———. *The Black Hills Journals of Colonel Richard Irving Dodge.* Edited by Wayne R. Kime. Norman: University of Oklahoma Press, 1996.

———. *A Living Issue.* Washington, D.C.: F. B. Mohun, 1882.

———. *Our Wild Indians: Thirty-three Years' Personal Experience among the Red Men of the Great West. A Popular Account of Their Social Life, Religion, Habits, Traits, Customs, Exploits, Etc. With Thrilling Adventures and Experiences on the Great Plains and in the Mountains of Our Wide Frontier.* Hartford: A. D. Worthington and Co., 1882.

———. *The Plains of North America and Their Inhabitants.* Edited by Wayne R. Kime. Newark: University of Delaware Press, 1989.

Dunlay, Thomas W. *Wolves for the Blue Soldiers: Indian Scouts and Auxiliaries with the United States Army.* Lincoln: University of Nebraska Press, 1982.

Ellis, Richard N. *General Pope and U. S. Indian Policy.* Albuquerque: University of New Mexico Press, 1970.

Farrow, Edward S. *Farrow's Military Encyclopedia: A Dictionary of Military Knowledge.* 2nd ed. 3 vols. New York: Military-Naval Publishing Co., 1895.

Finerty, John F. *War-Path and Bivouac: or, The Conquest of the Sioux.* Introduction by Oliver Knight. Norman: University of Oklahoma Press, 1961.

Foner, Jack D. *The United States Soldier between Two Wars: Army Life and Reforms, 1865–1898.* New York: Humanities Press, 1970.

Frazer, Robert W. *Forts of the West: Military Forts and Presidios and Posts Commonly Called Forts West of the Mississippi River to 1898.* Norman: University of Oklahoma Press, 1965.

Gray, John S. *Centennial Campaign: The Sioux War of 1876.* Fort Collins, Colo.: Old Army Press, 1976.

Greene, Jerome A. *Battles and Skirmishes of the Great Sioux War, 1876–1877: The Military View.* Norman: University of Oklahoma Press, 1993.

———. *Lakota and Cheyenne: Indian Views of the Great Sioux War, 1876–1877.* Norman: University of Oklahoma Press, 1994.

———. *Slim Buttes, 1876: An Episode of the Great Sioux War.* Norman: University of Oklahoma Press, 1982.

———. *Yellowstone Command: Colonel Nelson A. Miles and the Great Sioux War, 1876–77*. Lincoln: University of Nebraska Press, 1991.

Grinnell, George Bird. *The Fighting Cheyennes*. Norman: University of Oklahoma Press, 1956.

———. *Two Great Scouts and Their Pawnee Battalion: The Experiences of Frank J. North and Luther H. North, Pioneers in the Great West, 1856#1882, and Their Defence of the Building of the Union Pacific Railroad*. Cleveland: Arthur H. Clark Co., 1928.

Hamersley, L. R., comp. *Records of Living Officers of the United States Army*. Philadelphia: L. R. Hamersley and Co., 1884.

Hamersley, Thomas H., comp. *Complete Regular Army Register of the United States: For One Hundred Years (1779 to 1879)*. 2 vols. Washington, D.C.: T. Hamersley, 1880.

Hedren, Paul L. *Fort Laramie in 1876: Chronicle of a Frontier Post at War*. Lincoln: University of Nebraska Press, 1988.

———. *Traveler's Guide to the Great Sioux War: The Battlefields, Forts and Related Sites of America's Greatest Indian War*. Helena: Montana Historical Society Press, 1996.

Hedren, Paul L., ed. *The Great Sioux War, 1876–77: The Best from "Montana, the Magazine of Western History."* Helena: Montana Historical Society Press, 1991.

Heitman, Francis B. *Historical Register and Dictionary of the United States Army*. 2 vols. Washington, D.C.: Government Printing Office, 1903.

Hooker, William Francis. *The Bullwhacker: Adventures of a Frontier Freighter*. Introduction by David Dary. Edited by Howard R. Driggs. Lincoln: University of Nebraska Press, 1988.

Hughes, Richard B. *Pioneer Years in the Black Hills*. Edited by Agnes Wright Spring. Glendale, Calif.: Arthur H. Clark Co., 1957.

Hunton, John. *Diary*. Edited by L. G. (Pat) Flannery. Vol. 2. *1876–'77*. Lingle, Wyo.: Guide-Review, 1958.

Hutton, Paul A. *Phil Sheridan and His Army*. Lincoln: University of Nebraska Press, 1985.

Hutton, Paul A., ed. *Soldiers West: Biographies from the Military Frontier*. Introduction by Robert M. Utley. Lincoln: University of Nebraska Press, 1987.

Hyde, George E. *The Pawnee Indians*. Norman: University of Oklahoma Press, 1974.

Jackson, Donald. *Custer's Gold: The United States Cavalry Expedition of 1874*. New Haven: Yale University Press, 1966.

King, Charles. *Campaigning with Crook and Stories of Army Life*. New York: Harper and Brothers, 1890.

Knight, Oliver. *Following the Indian Wars: The Story of the Newspaper Correspondents among the Indian Campaigners*. Norman: University of Oklahoma Press, 1960.

———. *Life and Manners in the Frontier Army*. Norman: University of Oklahoma Press, 1960.

McChristian, Douglas C. *The U.S. Army in the West, 1870–1880: Uniforms, Weapons, and Equipment*. Norman: University of Oklahoma Press, 1995.

Miles, Nelson A. *Personal Recollections and Observations of General Nelson A. Miles*. Introduction by Robert M. Utley. New York: Da Capo Press, 1969.

Murray, Robert A. *Military Posts in the Powder River Country of Wyoming, 1865–1904*. Lincoln: University of Nebraska Press, 1968.

Newton, Henry W., and Walter P. Jenney. *Report on the Geology and Resources of the Black Hills of Dakota, With Atlas*. 2 vols. Washington, D.C.: Government Printing Office, 1880.

Nohl, Lessing J. "Bad Hand: The Military Career of Ranald Slidell Mackenzie, 1871–1889." Ph.D. diss., University of New Mexico, 1962.

Olson, James C. *Red Cloud and the Sioux Problem*. Lincoln: University of Nebraska Press, 1965.

Parker, Watson. *Gold in the Black Hills*. Norman: University of Oklahoma Press, 1966.

Pierce, Michael D. *The Most Promising Young Officer: A Life of Ranald Slidell Mackenzie*. Norman: University of Oklahoma Press, 1993.

Porter, Joseph C. *Paper Medicine Man: John Gregory Bourke and His American West*. Norman: University of Oklahoma Press, 1986.

Powell, Peter J. *People of the Sacred Mountain: A History of the Northern Cheyenne Chiefs and Warrior Societies*. 2 vols. San Francisco: Harper and Row, 1979.

———. *Sweet Medicine: The Continuing Role of the Sacred Arrows, the Sun Dance, and the Sacred Buffalo Hat in Northern Cheyenne History.* 2 vols. Norman: University of Oklahoma Press, 1969.

Record of Engagements with Hostile Indians within the Military Division of the Missouri, from 1868 to 1882, Lieutenant General P. H. Sheridan, Commanding. Washington, D.C.: Government Printing Office, 1882.

Rickey, Don, Jr. *Forty Miles a Day on Beans and Hay: The Enlisted Soldier Fighting the Indian Wars.* Norman: University of Oklahoma Press, 1963.

Roberts, Robert B. *Encyclopedia of Historic Forts: The Military, Pioneer, and Trading Posts of the United States.* New York: Macmillan, 1988.

Robinson, Charles M., III. *Bad Hand: A Biography of General Ranald S. Mackenzie.* Austin, Texas: State House Press, 1993.

———. *A Good Year to Die: The Story of the Great Sioux War.* New York: Random House, 1995.

Sandoz, Mari. *Crazy Horse, the Strange Man of the Oglalas: A Biography.* New York: Hastings House, 1942.

Schubert, Frank N. *Buffalo Soldiers, Braves, and the Brass.* Shippensburg, Pa.: White Mane Publishing Co., 1993.

Smith, Sherry L. *Sagebrush Soldier: Private William Earl Smith's View of the Sioux War of 1876.* Norman: University of Oklahoma Press, 1989.

Sorensen, Alfred R. *History of Omaha from the Pioneer Days to the Present Time.* Omaha: Gibson, Miller, and Richardson, 1889.

Stanton, W. S. *Tables of Distances and Itineraries of Routes Between the Military Posts in, and to Certain Points Contiguous to, the Department of the Platte.* Omaha: Headquarters, Department of the Platte, 1877.

Storm, Colton. *A Catalogue of the Everett D. Graff Collection of Western Americana.* Chicago: University of Chicago Press for the Newberry Library, 1968.

Turchen, Lesta V., and James D. McLaird. *The Black Hills Expedition of 1875.* Mitchell, S.D.: Dakota Wesleyan University Press, 1975.

Twenty-seventh Annual Reunion of the Association of Graduates of the United States Military Academy, at West Point, New York. Saginaw, Mich.: Seeman, Peters, 1896.

Utley, Robert M. *Frontier Regulars: The United States Army and the Indian, 1866–1891.* New York: Macmillan, 1973.

———. *The Lance and the Shield: The Life and Times of Sitting Bull.* New York: Henry Holt and Co., 1993.

Vaughn, Jesse W. *Indian Fights: New Facts on Seven Encounters.* Norman: University of Oklahoma Press, 1966.

———. *The Reynolds Campaign on Powder River.* Norman: University of Oklahoma Press, 1961.

———. *Sitting Bull, Champion of the Sioux.* 3rd ed. Introduction by Raymond J. DeMallie. Norman: University of Oklahoma Press, 1957.

———. *With Crook at the Rosebud.* Harrisburg, Pa.: Stackpole Co., 1956.

Walker, Henry Pickering. *The Wagonmasters: High Plains Freighting from the Earliest Days of the Santa Fe Trail to 1880.* Norman: University of Oklahoma Press, 1966.

Young, Harry (Sam). *Hard Knocks: A Life Story of the Vanishing West.* Portland: Wells, 1915.

Index

The following abbreviations are used in the index:
RID Richard Irving Dodge
PNA The Plains of North America and Their Inhabitants
PRE Powder River Expedition
References to maps and drawings are printed in **boldface** type.

CPSIA information can be obtained
at www.ICGtesting.com
Printed in the USA
FSOW01n0231131115
13341FS

9 780806 151854